SO-ACB-628

90252A

Debian
GNU/Linux
Guide to Installation and Usage

John Goerzen and Ossama Othman

New
Riders

201 West 103rd Street, Indianapolis, IN 46290

Debian GNU/Linux: Guide to Installation and Usage

Copyright © 1999 Software in the Public Interest and individual contributors

Permission is granted to make and distribute verbatim copies of this manual provided that the copyright notice and this permission notice are preserved on all copies.

Permission is granted to copy and distribute modified versions of this manual under the conditions for verbatim copying under the terms of the GNU General Public License as published by the Free Software Foundation—either version 2 of the License or (at your option) any later version.

Permission is granted to copy and distribute translations of this manual into another language under the conditions for modified versions under the terms of the GNU General Public License as published by the Free Software Foundation—either version 2 of the License or (at your option) any later version.

This work is distributed in the hope that it will be useful, but *without any warranty;* without even the implied warranty of *merchantability* or *fitness for a particular purpose.* See the GNU General Public License for more details.

See Appendix D for a copy of the GNU General Public License, or write to the Free Software Foundation, Inc., 59 Temple Place, Suite 330, Boston MA 02111-1307, USA.

International Standard Book Number: 0-7357-0914-9

Library of Congress Catalog Card Number: 99-63583

Printed in the United States of America

First Printing: July, 1999

03 02 01 00 99   7 6 5 4 3 2 1

Interpretation of the printing code: The rightmost double-digit number is the year of the book's printing; the rightmost single-digit number is the number of the book's printing. For example, the printing code 99-1 shows that the first printing of the book occurred in 1999.

Executive Editor
Laurie Petrycki

Managing Editor
Sarah Kearns

Project Editor
Alissa Cayton

Copy Editors
Gayle Johnson
Audra McFarland

Indexer
Tim Wright

Technical Editors
Ben Collins
Havoc Pennington

Trademarks

All terms mentioned in this book that are known to be trademarks or service marks have been appropriately capitalized. New Riders Publishing cannot attest to the accuracy of this information. Use of a term in this book should not be regarded as affecting the validity of any trademark or service mark.

Warning and Disclaimer

Every effort has been made to make this book as complete and accurate as possible, but no warranty or fitness is implied. The information provided is on an "as is" basis. The authors and the publisher shall have neither liability nor responsibility to any person or entity with respect to any loss or damages arising from the information contained in this book or from the use of the CD or programs accompanying it.

Contents at a Glance

Table of Contents

Preface

Freedom is still the most radical idea of all.

This quote, penned by Nathaniel Branden, seems fitting nowhere more so than with the freewheeling computing industry. In the space of just a few decades, lives the world over have been changed by computing technology. We, the people behind the Free Software movement, are seeking to continue this trend by truly opening up software to everyone—not just the few people working for the companies that write it—but everyone. As part of this goal, this book and CD contain a treasure chest of Free Software. Over one thousand packages, including things such as the world's most popular web server, can be found here. You can use this software for everything from graphic design to SQL databases.

The Free Software revolution has taken the industry by storm. Linux, started from scratch not even 10 years ago, has been the favorite kernel of the Free Software world. The ideas and experience gained from Free Software have truly sent Linux and the Free Software Foundation's GNU tools all over the world. Free systems such as Debian GNU/Linux ship with literally thousands of applications, and they have more power and stability and outperform some of the industry's traditional best-selling proprietary operating systems.

Today, GNU/Linux plays a dominant role in Internet servers and among ISPs, in academia, among computer hobbyists, and in computer science research. Debian GNU/Linux has brought the power of Free Software to everything from laptops to flights aboard the space shuttle. As I write this, companies the world over are experiencing the joy and benefits that are Free Software. The unprecedented power, the ability to speak directly to the people who write the software you use, the capability to modify programs at will, and the phenomenal expertise of the online support mechanism all combine to make Free Software a vibrant and wonderful way to use your computing resources.

Starting with a Free Software such as Debian GNU/Linux can be the best thing you've done with your computer in a long time. It's fast, powerful, stable, versatile, and fun! Welcome to the revolution!

—John Goerzen

About the Authors

John Goerzen has been a developer for Debian GNU/Linux for the past three years. Because Free Software has always been one of his interests, he is involved with several Free Software projects, including those outside the Debian circles. He currently works as a UNIX system administrator and developer for a regional ISP.

Ossama Othman is a member of the Center for Distributed Object Computing at Washington University in St. Louis, Missouri, where he researches Real-Time CORBA with the Center's CORBA object request broker TAO. He is also an active member of the Debian GNU/Linux organization and contributes regularly to the Open Source community.

Acknowledgments

Many people have helped with this manual. We'd like to thank everyone involved, and we try to do that here.

Thanks to Havoc Pennington, Ardo van Rangelrooij, Larry Greenfield, Thalia Hooker, Day Irmiter, James Treacy, Craig Sawyer, Oliver Elphick, Ivan E. Moore II, Eric Fischer, Mike Touloumtzis, and the Linux Documentation Project for their work on what became the Debian Tutorial document.

Thanks to Richard Stallman of the Free Software Foundation for advice and editing.

Thanks to Bruce Perens, Sven Rudolph, Igor Grobman, James Treacy, Adam Di Carlo, Tapio Lehtonen, and Stephane Bortzmeyer for their work on what became a collection of installation documents.

Of course, it's impossible to thank the hundreds of Debian developers and thousands of free software authors who gave us something to write about and use.

Tell Us What You Think!

As the reader of this book, you are our most important critic and commentator. We value your opinion, and we want to know what we're doing right, what we could do better, what areas you'd like to see us publish in, and any other words of wisdom you're willing to pass our way.

As an Executive Editor at New Riders Publishing, I welcome your comments. You can fax, email, or write me directly to let me know what you did or didn't like about this book—as well as what we can do to make our books stronger.

Please note that I cannot help you with technical problems related to the topic of this book, and that due to the high volume of mail I receive, I might not be able to reply to every message.

When you write, please be sure to include this book's title and author, as well as your name and phone or fax number. I will carefully review your comments and share them with the author and editors who worked on the book.

Fax: 317-581-4663
Email: newriders@mcp.com
Mail: Laurie Petrycki
            Executive Editor
            Networking
            New Riders Publishing
            201 West 103rd Street
            Indianapolis, IN 46290 USA

I

Guide

1

Introduction

We're glad to have this opportunity to introduce you to Debian! As we begin our journey down the road of GNU/Linux, we'd like to first talk a bit about what exactly Debian is – what it does, and how it fits in with the vast world of Free Software. Then, we talk a bit about the phenomenon that is Free Software and what it means for Debian and you. Finally, we close the chapter with a bit of information about this book itself.

1.1 What Is Debian?

Debian is a free operating system (OS) for your computer. An operating system is the set of basic programs and utilities that make your computer run. At the core of an operating system is the *kernel*. The kernel is the most fundamental program on the computer: It does all the basic housekeeping and lets you start other programs. Debian uses the *Linux* kernel, a completely free piece of software started by Linus Torvalds and supported by thousands of programmers worldwide. A large part of the basic tools that fill out the operating system come from the GNU Project[1], and these tools are also free.

Another facet of an operating system is application software: programs that help get work done, from editing documents to running a business to playing games to writing more software. Debian comes with more than 1,500 *packages* (precompiled software bundled up in a nice format for easy installation on your machine) – all for free.

The Debian system is a bit like a pyramid. At the base is Linux. On top of that are all the basic tools, mostly from GNU. Next is all the application software that you run on the computer; many of these are also from GNU. The Debian developers act as architects and coordinators – carefully organizing the system and fitting everything together into an integrated, stable operating system: Debian GNU/Linux.

The design philosophy of GNU/Linux is to distribute its functionality into small, multipurpose parts. That way, you can easily achieve new functionality and new features by combining the small parts (programs) in new ways. Debian is like an erector set: You can build all sorts of things with it.

When you're using an operating system, you want to minimize the amount of work you put into getting your job done. Debian supplies many tools that can help, but only if you know what these tools do. Spending an hour trying to get something to work and then finally giving up isn't very productive. This guide will teach you about the core tools that make up Debian: what tools to use in certain situations and how to tie these various tools together.

1.1.1   Who Creates Debian?

Debian is an all-volunteer Internet-based development project. There are hundreds of volunteers working on it. Most are in charge of a small number of software packages and are very familiar with the software they package.

These volunteers work together by following a strict set of guidelines governing how packages are assembled. These guidelines are developed cooperatively in discussions on Internet mailing lists.

---

1. http://www.gnu.org/

1.2   A Multiuser, Multitasking Operating System

As we mentioned earlier in section 1.1, the design of Debian GNU/Linux comes from the Unix operating system. Unlike common desktop operating systems such as DOS, Windows, and MacOS, GNU/Linux is usually found on large servers and *multiuser* systems.

This means that Debian has features those other operating systems lack. It allows a large number of people to use the same computer at once, as long as each user has his or her own *terminal*.[2] To permit many users to work at once, Debian must allow many programs and applications to run simultaneously. This feature is called *multitasking*.

Much of the power (and complexity) of GNU/Linux systems stems from these two features. For example, the system must have a way to keep users from accidentally deleting each other's files. The operating system also must coordinate the many programs running at once to ensure that they don't all use the same resource, such as a hard drive, at the same time.

If you keep in mind what Debian was originally designed to do, many aspects of it will make a lot more sense. You'll learn to take advantage of the power of these features.

1.3   What Is Free Software?

When Debian developers and users speak of "Free Software," they refer to *freedom* rather than price. Debian is free in this sense: You are free to modify and redistribute it and will always have access to the source code for this purpose. The Debian Free Software Guidelines[3] describe in more detail exactly what is meant by "free." The Free Software Foundation[4], originator of the GNU Project, is another excellent source of information. You can find a more detailed discussion of free software on the Debian web site[5]. One of the most well-known works in this field is Richard M. Stallman's essay, *Why Software Should Be Free*[6]; take a look at it for some insight into why we support Free Software as we do. Recently, some

---

2. A terminal is just a keyboard and a screen that are connected to the computer through the network, over a modem, or directly. Your keyboard and monitor form a terminal that is directly attached to the computer: This special terminal is often called the *console*.

3. http://www.debian.org/social_contract#guidelines

4. http://www.fsf.org/

5. http://www.debian.org/

6. http://www.fsf.org/philosophy/shouldbefree.html

people have started calling Free Software "Open Source Software"; the two terms are interchangable.

You may wonder why would people spend hours of their own time writing software and carefully packaging it, only to give it all away. The answers are as varied as the people who contribute.

Many believe in sharing information and having the freedom to cooperate with one another, and they feel that free software encourages this. A long tradition that upholds these values, sometimes called the Hacker[7] Ethic, started in the 1950s. The Debian GNU/Linux Project was founded based on these Free Software ethics of freedom, sharing, and cooperation.

Others want to learn more about computers. More and more people are looking for ways to avoid the inflated price of proprietary software. A growing community contributes in appreciation for all the great free software they've received from others.

Many in academia create free software to help get the results of their research into wider use. Businesses help maintain free software so they can have a say in how it develops – there's no quicker way to get a new feature than to implement it yourself or hire a consultant to do so! Business is also interested in greater reliability and the ability to choose between support vendors.

Still others see free software as a social good, democratizing access to information and preventing excessive centralization of the world's information infrastructure. Of course, a lot of us just find it great fun.

Debian is so committed to free software that we thought it would be useful if it was formalized in a document of some sort. Our Social Contract[8] promises that Debian will always be 100% free software. When you install a package from the Debian main distribution, you can be sure it meets our Free Software Guidelines.

Although Debian believes in free software, there are cases where people want to put proprietary software on their machine. Whenever possible Debian will support this; though proprietary software is not included in the main distribution, it is sometimes available on the FTP site in the `non-free` directory, and there is a growing number of packages whose sole job is to install proprietary software we are not allowed to distribute ourselves.

---

7. Note that the term "hacker" should not be confused with the term "cracker." In short, a hacker is benevolent, whereas a cracker is generally considered malevolent. Movies and other forms of media many times incorrectly use the term "hacker" instead of "cracker."

8. http://www.debian.org/social_contract

It is important to distinguish *commercial* software from *proprietary* software. Proprietary software is non-free software; commercial software is software sold for money. Debian permits commercial software, but not proprietary software, to be a part of the main distribution. Remember that the phrase "free software" does not refer to price; it is quite possible to sell free software. For more clarification of the terminology, see `http://www.opensource.org/` or `http://www.fsf.org/philosophy/categories.html`.

1.4   About This Book

This book is aimed at readers who are new to Debian GNU/Linux. It assumes no prior knowledge of GNU/Linux or other Unix-like systems, but it does assume very basic general knowledge about computers and hardware; you should know what the basic parts of a computer are, and what one might use a computer to do.

In general, this tutorial tries to help you understand what happens inside a Debian system. The idea is to empower you to solve new problems and get the most out of your computer. Thus there's plenty of theory and fun facts thrown in with the "How To" aspects of the manual.

We'd love to hear your comments about this book! You can reach the authors at `debian-guide@complete.org`. We're especially interested in whether it was helpful to you and how we could make it better. Whether you have a comment or think this book is the greatest thing since sliced bread, please send us e-mail.

Please do not send the authors technical questions about Debian, because there are other forums for that; see Appendix A on page 119 for more information on the documentation and getting help. Only send mail regarding the book itself to the above address.

1.4.1   How to Read This Book

The best way to learn about almost any computer program is by using it. Most people find that reading a book without using the program isn't beneficial. The best way to learn about Unix and GNU/Linux is by using them. Use GNU/Linux for everything you can. Feel free to experiment!

Debian isn't as intuitively obvious as some other operating systems. You will probably end up reading at least the first few chapters of this book. GNU/Linux's power and complexity make it difficult to approach at first, but far more rewarding in the long run.

The suggested way to learn is to read a little, and then play a little. Keep playing until you're comfortable with the concepts, and then start skipping around in the book. You'll find a variety of topics are covered,

some of which you might find interesting. After a while, you should feel
confident enough to start using commands without knowing exactly what
they do. This is a good thing.

> Tip: If you ever mistakenly type a command or don't know
> how to exit a program, press CTRL-c (the Ctrl key and the
> lowercase letter c pressed simultaneously). This will often stop
> the program.

1.4.2   Conventions

Before going on, it's important to be familiar with the typographical
conventions used in this book.

When you should simultaneously hold down multiple keys, a notation
like CTRL-a will be used. This means "press the Ctrl key and press
lowercase letter a." Some keyboards have both Alt and Meta; most home
computers have only Alt, but the Alt key behaves like a Meta key. So if
you have no Meta key, try the Alt key instead.

Keys like Alt and Meta are called *modifier* keys because they change
the meaning of standard keys like the letter A. Sometimes you need to
hold down more than one modifier; for example, Meta-Ctrl-a means to
simultaneously press Meta, Ctrl, and lowercase a.

Some keys have a special notation – for example, Ret (Return/Enter),
Del (Delete or sometimes Backspace), Esc (Escape). These should be
fairly self-explanatory.

Spaces used instead of hyphens mean to press the keys in sequential
order. For example, CTRL-a x RET means to simultaneously type Ctrl
and lowercase a, followed by the letter x, followed by pressing Return.
(On some keyboards, this key is labeled Enter. Same key, different name.)

In sample sessions, bold face text denotes characters typed by the
user, italicized text denotes comments about a given part of the sample
session, and all other text is output from entering a command. For shorter
commands, you'll sometimes find that the command can be found within
other text, highlighed with a monospace font.

Getting Started

> *"A journey of a thousand miles must begin with a single step."* – Lao-Tsu

Now that you've read about the ideas and philosophy behind Linux and Debian, it's time to start putting it on your computer! We start by talking about how to prepare for a Debian install, then about partitioning your disk, and finally, how to start up the installation system.

2.1 Supported Hardware

Debian does not impose hardware requirements beyond the requirements of the Linux kernel and the GNU tools.

Rather than attempting to describe all the different hardware configurations that are supported for the PC platform, this section contains general information and pointers to where additional information can be found.

There are two excellent places to check for detailed information: the Debian System Requirements[1] list and the Linux Documentation Project Hardware Compatibility HOWTO[2]. For information on video card support, you may also want to look at the XFree86[3] Project web site.

2.1.1   Memory and Disk Space Requirements

You must have at least 4MB of memory and 35MB of available hard disk space. If you want to install a reasonable amount of software, including the X Window system, and some development programs and libraries, you'll need at least 300MB. For an essentially full installation, you'll need around 800MB. To install *everything* available in Debian, you'll probably need around 2GB. Actually, installing everything doesn't make sense because some packages provide the same services.

2.2   Before You Start

Before you start, make sure to back up every file that is now on your system. The installation procedure can wipe out all of the data on a hard disk! The programs used in installation are quite reliable and most have seen years of use; still, a false move can cost you. Even after backing up, be careful and think about your answers and actions. Two minutes of thinking can save hours of unnecessary work.

Debian makes it possible to have both Debian GNU/Linux and another operating system installed on the same system. If you plan to use this option, make sure that you have on hand the original CD-ROM or floppies of the other installed operating systems. If you repartition your boot drive, you may find that you have to reinstall your existing operating system's boot loader[4] or the entire operating system itself.

2.2.1   Information You Will Need

If your computer is connected to a network 24 hours a day (i.e., an Ethernet or similar LAN connection – not a PPP connection), you should ask your network's system administrator for the following information:

- Your host name (you may be able to decide this on your own)
- Your domain name

---

1. http://www.debian.org/releases/slink/i386/ch-hardware-req.en.html
2. http://metalab.unc.edu/LDP/HOWTO/Hardware-HOWTO.html
3. http://www.xfree86.org/
4. A boot loader is responsible starting an operating system's boot procedure.

- Your computer's IP address
- The IP address of your network
- The netmask to use with your network
- The broadcast address to use on your network
- The IP address of the default gateway system you should route to, if your network *has* a gateway
- The system on your network that you should use as a DNS server
- Whether you connect to the network using Ethernet
- Whether your Ethernet interface is a PCMCIA card, and if so, the type of PCMCIA controller you have

If your only network connection is a telephone line using PPP or an equivalent dialup connection, you don't need to worry about getting your network set up until your system is already installed. See section 11.1 on page 99 for information on setting up PPP under Debian.

2.3   Partitioning Your Hard Drive

Before you install Debian on your computer, it is generally a good idea to plan how the contents of your hard drive will be arranged. One part of this process involves partitioning your hard drive.

2.3.1   Background

Partitioning your disk simply refers to the act of breaking up your disk into sections. Each section is then independent of the others. It's roughly equivalent to putting up walls in a house; after that, adding furniture to one room doesn't affect any other room.

If you already have an operating system on your system (Windows 95, Windows NT, DOS, etc.) and you want to install Debian GNU/Linux on the same disk, you will probably need to repartition the disk. In general, changing a partition that already has a filesystem on it will destroy any information in that filesystem. Therefore, you should always make backups before doing any repartitioning. Using the analogy of the house, you would probably want to move all the furniture out of the way before moving a wall or you risk destroying your furniture. Luckily, there is an alternative for some users; see section 2.3.6 on page 16 for more information.

At a bare minimum, GNU/Linux needs one partition for itself. You can have a single partition containing the entire operating system, applications, and your personal files. Most people choose to give GNU/Linux more than the minimum number of partitions, however.

There are two reasons you might want to break up the filesystem into a number of smaller partitions. The first is for safety. If something happens to corrupt the filesystem, generally only one partition is affected. Thus, you only have to replace (from the backups you've been carefully keeping) a portion of your system. At the very least, you should consider creating what is commonly called a "root partition." This contains the most essential components of the system. If any other partitions get corrupted, you can still boot into GNU/Linux to fix the system. This can save you the trouble of having to reinstall the system from scratch.

The second reason is generally more important in a business setting, but it really depends on your use of the machine. Suppose something runs out of control and starts eating disk space. If the process causing the problem happens to have root privileges (the system keeps a percentage of the disk away from users), you could suddenly find yourself out of disk space. This is not good since the operating system needs to use real files (besides swap space) for many things. It may not even be a problem of local origin. For example, unsolicited e-mail ("spam") can easily fill a partition. By using more partitions, you protect the system from many of these problems. Using e-mail as an example again, by putting the directory /var/spool/mail on its own partition, the bulk of the system will work even if unsolicited e-mail fills that partition.

Another reason applies only if you have a large IDE disk drive and are using neither LBA addressing nor overlay drivers[5]. In this case, you will have to put the root partition into the first 1,024 cylinders of your hard drive, usually around 524 megabytes. See section 2.3.3 on page 14 for more information on this issue.

Most people feel that a swap partition is also a necessity, although this isn't strictly true. "Swap" is scratch space for an operating system, which allows the system to use disk storage as "virtual memory" in addition to physical memory. Putting swap on a separate partition allows Linux to make much more efficient use of it. It is possible to force Linux to use a regular file as swap, but this is not recommended.

The only real drawback to using more partitions is that it is often difficult to know in advance what your needs will be. If you make a partition too small, either you will have to reinstall the system, or you will be constantly moving things around to make room in the undersized partition. On the other hand, if you make the partition too big, you may be wasting space that could be used elsewhere.

---

5. See your hard drive manual for a description of these features.

2.3.2   Planning Use of the System

Disk space requirements and your partitioning scheme are influenced by the type of installation you decide to create.

For your convenience, Debian offers a number of default "profiles" some of which are listed later in this section. Profiles are simply preselected sets of packages designed to provide certain desired capabilities on your system. Installation is easier since packages that fit your desired profile are automatically marked for installation. Each given profile lists the size of the resulting system after installation is complete. Even if you don't use these profiles, this discussion is important for planning, since it will give you a sense of how large your partition or partitions need to be. The following are some of the available profiles and their sizes:

Server_std. This is a small server profile, useful for a stripped-down server, that does not have a lot of niceties for shell users. It basically has an FTP server, a web server, DNS, NIS, and POP. It will take up around 50MB. Of course, this is just the size of the software; any data you serve would be additional.

Dialup. This profile would be good for a standard desktop box, including the X Window system, graphics applications, sound, editors, etc. The size of the packages will be around 500MB.

Work_std. This profile is suitable for a stripped-down user machine without the X Window system or X applications. It is also suitable for a laptop or mobile computer. The size is around 140MB. It is possible to have a simple laptop setup including X with less than 100MB.

Devel_comp. This is a desktop setup profile with all the popular development packages, such as Perl, C, and C++. It requires around 475MB. Assuming you are adding X and some additional packages for other uses, you should plan for approximately 800MB of disk space for this type of installation.

Remember that these sizes don't include all the other materials that are normally found, such as user files, mail, and data. It is always best to be generous when considering the space for your own files and data. Notably, the Debian /var directory contains a lot of state information. The installed package management files can easily consume 20MB of disk space. In general, you should allocate at least 50MB for the /var directory because system log files are also stored there.

2.3.3   PC Disk Limitations

A PC BIOS generally adds additional constraints for disk partitioning. There is a limit to how many "primary" and "logical" partitions a drive can contain. Additionally, there are limits to where on the drive the BIOS looks for boot information. More information can be found in the Linux Partition mini-HOWTO[6]. This section will include a brief overview to help you plan most situations.

"Primary" partitions are the original partitioning scheme for PC hard disks. However, there can be only four of them. To get past this limitation, "extended" or "logical" partitions were invented. By setting one of your primary partitions as an extended partition, you can subdivide all the space allocated to that partition into logical partitions. The number of logical partitions you can create is much less limited than the number of primary partitions you can create; however, you can have only one extended partition per drive.

Linux limits the number of partitions per drive to 15 partitions for SCSI drives (3 usable primary partitions, 12 logical partitions), and 63 partitions for IDE drives (3 usable primary partitions, 60 logical partitions).

The last issue you need to know about a PC BIOS is that your boot partition – that is, the partition containing your kernel image – needs to be contained within the first 1,024 cylinders of the drive. Because the root partition is usually your boot partition, you need to make sure your root partition fits into the first 1,024 cylinders.

If you have a large disk, you may have to use cylinder translation techniques, which you can set in your BIOS, such as LBA translation mode. (More information about large disks can be found in the Large Disk mini-HOWTO[7].) If you are using a cylinder translation scheme, your boot partition must fit within the *translated* representation of cylinder 1,024.

2.3.4   Device Names in Linux

Linux disks and partition names may be different from those in other operating systems. You should know the names that Linux uses when you create and mount partitions. The basic scheme can be found in Table 2.1 on page 15.

The partitions on each disk are represented by appending a number to the disk name. For example, the names **hda1** and **hda2** represent the first

---

6. http://metalab.unc.edu/LDP/HOWTO/mini/Partition.html
7. http://metalab.unc.edu/LDP/HOWTO/mini/Large-Disk.html

Table 2.1   Linux Device Names

Device	Linux Name
First floppy drive	/dev/fd0
Second floppy drive ·	/dev/fd1
First partition on /dev/hda (typically C: in other OSs)	/dev/hda1
Fifth partition on /dev/hdc	/dev/hdc5
Second partition on /dev/sdb	/dev/sdb2
Entire Primary-Master IDE hard disk or CD-ROM	/dev/hda
Entire Primary-Slave IDE hard disk or CD-ROM	/dev/hdb
Entire Secondary-Master IDE hard disk or CD-ROM	/dev/hdc
Entire Secondary-Slave IDE hard disk or CD-ROM	/dev/hdd
First SCSI disk	/dev/sda
Second and remaining SCSI disks	/dev/sdb and so forth
First serial port (COM1 in other OSs)	/dev/ttyS0
Second, third, etc. serial ports	/dev/ttyS1, /dev/ttyS2, etc.
SCSI tape units (automatic rewind)	/dev/st0, /dev/st1, etc.
SCSI tape units (no automatic rewind)	/dev/nst0, /dev/nst1, etc.
SCSI CD-ROMs	/dev/scd0, /dev/scd1, etc.

and second partitions of the first IDE disk drive in your system. Linux represents the primary partitions with the drive name plus the numbers 1 through 4. For example, the first primary partition on the first IDE drive is **/dev/hda1**. The logical partitions are numbered starting at 5, so the first logical partition on that same drive is **/dev/hda5**. Remember that the extended partition – that is, the primary partition holding the logical partitions – is not usable by itself. This applies to SCSI drives as well as IDE drives.

Let's assume you have a system with two SCSI disks, one at SCSI address 2 and the other at SCSI address 4. The first disk (at address 2) is then named **sda** and the second **sdb**. If the **sda** drive has three partitions on it, these will be named **sda1**, **sda2**, and **sda3**. The same applies to the **sdb** disk and its partitions. Note that if you have two SCSI host bus adapters (i.e., controllers), the order of the drives can get confusing. The best solution in this case is to watch the boot messages, assuming you know the drive models.

2.3.5 Recommended Partitioning Scheme

As described above, you should have a separate smaller root partition and a larger /usr partition if you have the space. For most users, the two partitions initially mentioned are sufficient. This is especially appropriate when you have a single small disk, because creating lots of partitions can waste space.

In some cases, you might need a separate /usr/local partition if you plan to install many programs that are not part of the Debian distribution. If your machine will be a mail server, you may need to make /var/spool/mail a separate partition. Putting /tmp on its own 20 to 32MB partition, for instance, is a good idea. If you are setting up a server with lots of user accounts, it's generally good to have a separate, large /home partition to store user home directories. In general, the partitioning situation varies from computer to computer depending on its uses.

For very complex systems, you should see the Multi Disk HOWTO[8]. It contains in-depth information, mostly of interest to people setting up servers.

Swap partition sizes should also be considered. There are many views about swap partition sizes. One rule of thumb that works well is to use as much swap as you have system memory, although there probably isn't much point in going over 64MB of swap for most users. It also shouldn't be smaller than 16MB, in most cases. Of course, there are exceptions to these rules. If you are trying to solve 10,000 simultaneous equations on a machine with 256MB of memory, you may need a gigabyte (or more) of swap space.

As an example, consider a machine that has 32MB of RAM and a 1.7GB IDE drive on /dev/hda. There is a 500MB partition for another operating system on /dev/hda1. A 32MB swap partition is used on /dev/hda3 and the rest, about 1.2GB, on /dev/hda2 is the Linux partition.

2.3.6 Partitioning Prior to Installation

There are two different times that you can partition: prior to or during the installation of Debian. If your computer will be solely dedicated to Debian you should partition during installation as described in section 3.5 on page 25. If you have a machine with more than one operating system on it, you should generally let the other operating system create its own partitions.

---

8. http://metalab.unc.edu/LDP/HOWTO/Multi-Disk-HOWTO.html

The following sections contain information regarding partitioning in your native operating system prior to Debian installation. Note that you'll have to map between how the other operating system names partitions and how Linux names partitions; see Table 2.1 on page 15.

Partitioning from DOS or Windows

If you are manipulating existing FAT or NTFS partitions, it is recommended that you use either the scheme below or native Windows or DOS tools. Otherwise, it is not really necessary to partition from DOS or Windows; the Linux partitioning tools will generally do a better job.

Lossless Repartitioning

One of the most common installations is onto a system that already contains DOS (including Windows 3.1), Win32 (such as Windows 95, 98, NT), or OS/2 and it is desired to put Debian onto the same disk without destroying the previous system. As explained in section 2.3.1 on page 11, decreasing the size of an existing partition will almost certainly damage the data on that partition unless certain precautions are taken. The method described here, while not guaranteed to protect your data, works extremely well in practice. As a precaution, you should *make a backup.*

Before going any further, you should have decided how you will divide up the disk. The method in this section will only split a partition into two pieces. One will contain the original operating system, and the other will be used for Debian. During the installation of Debian, you will be given the opportunity to use the Debian portion of the disk as you see fit, i.e., as swap or as a filesystem.

The idea is to move all the data on the partition to the beginning before changing the partition information, so that nothing will be lost. It is important that you do as little as possible between the data movement and repartitioning to minimize the chance of a file being written near the end of the partition as this will decrease the amount of space you can take from the partition.

The first thing you need is a copy of FIPS, which is available in the **tools** directory on your Debian CD-ROM. This disk must be bootable. Under DOS, a bootable floppy can be created using the command **sys a:** for a previously formatted floppy or **format a: /s** for an unformatted floppy. Unzip the archive and copy the files **RESTORRB.EXE**, **FIPS.EXE** and **ERRORS.TXT** to the bootable floppy. FIPS comes with very good documentation that you may want to read. You should definitely read the documentation if you use a disk compression driver or a disk manager. Create the disk and read the documentation *before* you continue.

The next thing to be done is to move all the data to the beginning of the partition. DEFRAG, which comes standard with DOS 6.0 and later, can easily do the job. See the FIPS documentation for a list of other software that may also work. Note that if you have Windows 95 or higher, you must run DEFRAG from there, because DOS doesn't understand VFAT, which is used to support long filenames in Windows 95 and higher.

After running the defragmenter (which can take a while on a large disk), reboot with the FIPS floppy disk you created. Simply type a:\ fips and follow the directions.

Note that there are many other other partition managers out there, in case FIPS doesn't work for you.

2.3.7   Debian Installation Steps

As you initially install Debian, you will proceed through several different steps:

1. Boot the installation system
2. Initial system configuration
3. Install the base system
4. Boot the newly installed base system
5. Install the rest of the system

Booting the Debian installation system, the first step, is generally done with the Rescue Floppy or from the CD-ROM.

Once you've booted into Linux, the dbootstrap program will launch and guide you through the second step, the initial system configuration. This step is described in detail in section 3 on page 23.

The "Debian base system" is a core set of packages that are required to run Debian in a minimal, stand-alone fashion. dbootstrap will install it from your CD-ROM, as described in section 3.12 on page 30. Once you have configured and installed the base system, your machine can "stand on its own."

The final step is the installation of the remainder of the Debian system. This would include the applications and documents that you actually use on your computer, such as the X Window system, editors, shells, and development environments. The rest of the Debian system can be installed from CD-ROM. At this point, you'll be using the standard Debian package management tools, such as dselect. This step is described in section 3.20 on page 34.

2.4   Choosing Your Installation Media

First, choose the boot media for the installation system. Next, choose the method you will use to install the base system.

To boot the installation system, you have the following choices: bootable CD-ROM, floppies, or a non-Linux boot loader.

CD-ROM booting is one of the easiest ways to install. Not all machines can boot directly from the CD-ROM so you may still need to use floppies. Booting from floppies is supported for most platforms. Floppy booting is described in section 2.4.2 on page 19.

2.4.1   Installing from a CD-ROM

If your system supports booting from a CD-ROM, you don't need any floppies. Put the CD-ROM into the drive, turn your computer off, and then turn it back on. You should see a Welcome screen with a boot prompt at the bottom. Now you can skip down to section 2.5.

If your computer didn't "see" the Debian CD-ROM, the easiest option is to make two floppies for booting (described in section 2.4.2) and then use them to start Debian. Don't worry; after Debian is finished with those two floppies, it will find your CD-ROM with no trouble.

2.4.2   Booting from Floppies

It's not hard at all to boot from floppies. In fact, your CD-ROM contains all the information necessary to create boot disks for you. For these instructions, you will need to get two disks. Label the first one "Debian 2.1 Install/Rescue Disk" and the second "Debian 2.1 Modules/Drivers Disk."

Creating Floppies from Disk Images

Disk images are files containing the complete contents of a floppy disk in *raw* form. Disk images, such as `resc1440.bin`, cannot simply be copied to floppy drives. A special program is used to write the image files to floppy disk in *raw* mode.

First, you need to get to a DOS prompt. In Windows 95 and above, you can do this by double-clicking on an MS-DOS icon or by going to Start→Programs→MS-DOS prompt. Then, insert your Debian GNU/Linux CD-ROM into your CD-ROM drive. First, you change to your CD-ROM drive. In most cases, this is D:.

```
C:\WINDOWS>D:
```

Now, change to the directory containing the disk images.

```
D:\>CD
\DISTS\SLINK\MAIN\DISKS-I386\2.1.8-1999-02-22
```

If you get an error, double-check what you're typing. If the error persists, manually issue CD \DISTS\SLINK\MAIN\DISKS-I386, then run DIR, and then CD into the directory indicated. Note that the above commands, and some other examples below, may appear as a single line on your display even if they are wrapped here.

Now, you're ready to create the first of two disks. Start the program to write them out, rawrite2:

```
D:\DISTS\SLINK\MAIN\DISKS-I386\
2.1.8-1999-02-22>rawrite2
RaWrite 2.0 - Write disk file to
raw floppy diskette
```

Rawrite2 starts and displays its welcome message. Next, it asks for the filename and diskette drive. You tell it to write resc1440.bin to a:

```
Enter disk image source file name: resc1440.bin
Enter target diskette drive: a:
```

Rawrite2 now asks you to insert a disk into the floppy drive. Do so and press Enter.

```
Plese insert a formatted diskette into
drive A: and press -ENTER- :
```

At this point, rawrite2 will create the first of the two disks. Now, you need to repeat the process for the second disk:

```
D:\DISTS\SLINK\MAIN\DISKS-I386\
2.1.8-1999-02-22>rawrite2
RaWrite 2.0 - Write disk file to
raw floppy diskette
Enter disk image source file name: drv1440.bin
Enter target diskette drive: a:
Please insert a formatted diskette into
drive A: and press -ENTER- :
```

By now, your disks are created. You can now use the first one to boot.

Booting Debian

You are now ready to boot into Debian! Shut down your existing operating system, turn off your computer, and place the Install/Rescue Disk into the floppy drive. Now turn your computer back on. You should get a Welcome screen with a boot prompt at the bottom.

2.5   Booting the Installation System

You should now have the `boot` prompt. Simply press `Enter` at this point.

Once you press `Enter`, you should see the message `Loading...`, and then `Uncompressing Linux...`, and then a screenful or so of information about the hardware in your system. In general, you can ignore these messages. Linux will look for various hardware devices and will tell you what it finds and doesn't find. Don't worry about messages at this point. Just wait until you see the Color Selection screen. If you have trouble, see section B.2 on page 127.

3

Step-by-Step Installation

dbootstrap is the name of the program that is run after you have booted into the installation system. It is responsible for initial system configuration and the installation of the "base system."

The main job of dbootstrap and the main purpose of your initial system configuration is to configure certain core elements of your system. For instance, this includes your IP address, host name, and other aspects of your networking setup, if any. This also includes the configuration of "kernel modules," which are drivers that are loaded into the kernel. These modules include storage hardware drivers, network drivers, special language support, and support for other peripherals. Configuring these fundamental things is done first, because it is often necessary for the system to function properly for the next steps of installation.

dbootstrap is a simple, character-based application. It is very easy to use; generally, it will guide you through each step of the installation process in a linear fashion. You can also go back and repeat steps if you made a mistake. Navigation within dbootstrap is accomplished with the arrow keys, Enter, and Tab.

3.1   Select Color or Monochrome Display

Once the system has finished booting, dbootstrap is invoked. The first thing that dbootstrap asks about is your display. You should see the "Select Color or Monochrome display" dialog box. If your monitor is capable of displaying color, press Enter. The display should change from black-and-white to color. Then press Enter again, on the "Next" item, to continue with the installation.

If your monitor can display only black and white, use the arrow keys to move the cursor to the "Next" menu item, and then press Enter to continue with the installation.

3.2   Debian GNU/Linux Installation Main Menu

You may see a dialog box that says "The installation program is determining the current state of your system and the next installation step that should be performed." This is a phase in which the installation program automatically figures out what you probably need to do next. In some cases, you may not even see this box.

During the entire installation process, you will be presented with the main menu, titled "Debian GNU/Linux Installation Main Menu." The choices at the top of the menu will change to indicate your progress in installing the system. Phil Hughes wrote in the *Linux Journal*[1] that you could teach a *chicken* to install Debian! He meant that the installation process was mostly just *pecking* at the *Enter* key. The first choice on the installation menu is the next action that you should perform according to what the system detects you have already done. It should say "Next," and at this point the next step in installing the system will be taken.

3.3   Configure the Keyboard

Make sure the highlight is on the "Next" item and press Enter to go to the keyboard configuration menu.

Move the highlight to the keyboard selection you desire and press Enter. Use the arrow keys to move the highlight. In most cases, you can just use the default U.S. layout.

---

1. http://www.linuxjournal.com

3.4   Last Chance to Back Up!

Did we tell you to back up your disks? Here's your first chance to wipe out all of the data on your disks and your last chance to save your old system. If you haven't backed up all of your disks, remove the floppy from the drive, reset the system, and run backups.

3.5   Partition a Hard Disk

Whatever the "Next" menu selection is, you can use the down-arrow key to select "Partition a Hard Disk." Go ahead and do this now, then press Enter.

The "Partition a Hard Disk" menu item presents you with a list of disk drives you can partition and runs a partitioning application called cfdisk. You must create at least one "Linux native" (type 83) disk partition, and you probably want at least one "Linux swap" (type 82) partition, as explained in later in this section.

You will now create the partitions that you need to install Debian. For this example, the assumption is that you are partitioning an empty hard disk.

The boot partition must reside within the first 1,024 of cylinders of your hard disk (see section 2.3.3 on page 14). Keeping that in mind, use the right-arrow key to highlight the "New" menu selection, and then press Enter. You will be presented with the choice of creating a *primary* partition or a *logical* partition. To help ensure that the partition containing the boot information is within the first 1,024 cylinders, create a primary partition first. This primary partition will be your "Linux native" partition.

Highlight the "Primary" menu selection and press Enter. Next you will need to enter how large you want that partition to be. Review section 2.3.2 on page 13 if you're not sure how large it should be. Remember to leave enough space for your swap partition (see section 2.3.5 on page 16). Enter the parition size you want and then press Enter. Next you will be asked if you want to place the partition at the beginning of free space or at the end. Place it at the beginning to help ensure that it lies within the first 1,024 cylinders. Highlight "Beginning" and press Enter. At this point you will be brought back to the main screen. Notice that the partition you created is listed. By default, a Linux native partition was created. This partition must now be made bootable. Make sure that the "Bootable" menu selection is highlighted and press Enter. The partition should now have the word "Boot" listed under the "Flags" column.

With the remaining space, create another primary partition. Using the down-arrow key, highlight the *free space* entry in the partition list. Now

Figure 3.1 `cfdisk` screenshot

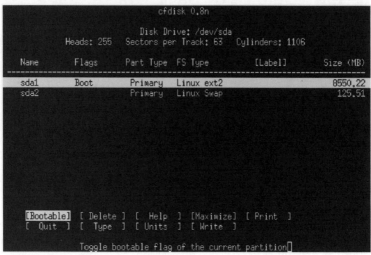

highlight the "New" menu selection and proceed just as you did when you created the first primary partition. Notice that the partition is listed as a Linux native partition. Because this partition will be your swap partition, it must be denoted as such. Make sure the partition you just created (your swap partition) is highlighted and then press the left-arrow key until the "Type" menu selection is highlighted, then press Enter. You will be presented with a list of supported partition types. The Linux swap partition type should already be selected. If it is not, enter the number from the list that corresponds to the Linux swap partition (82), and then press Enter. Your swap partition should now be listed as a Linux swap partition under the "FS Type" column in the main screen.

Your `cfdisk` screen should look something like the screenshot in Figure 3.1 on page 26. The numbers may not be the same, but the Flags and FS Type column shoulds be similar.

Until now, nothing on your disk has been altered. If you are satisfied that the partition scheme you created is what you want, press the left-arrow key until "Write" is highlighted, and press Enter. Your hard disk has now been partitioned. Quit the `cfdisk` application by selecting the "Quit" menu selection. Once you have left `cfdisk`, you should be back in Debian's `dbootstrap` installation application.

3.6   Initialize and Activate a Swap Partition

This will be the "Next" menu item once you have created one disk partition. You have the choice of initializing and activating a new swap partition, activating a previously-initialized one, or doing without a swap partition.

A swap partition is strongly recommended, but you can do without one if you insist and if your system has more than 4MB RAM. If you wish to do this, select the "Do Without a Swap Partition" item from the menu and move on to the next section.

It's always permissible to reinitialize a swap partition, so select "Initialize and Activate a Swap Partition" unless you are sure you know what you are doing. This menu choice will first present you with a dialog box reading "Please select the partition to activate as a swap device." The default device presented should be the swap partition you've already set up; if so, just press Enter.

Next you have the option to scan the entire partition for unreadable disk blocks caused by defects on the surface of the hard disk platters. This is useful if you have MFM, RLL, or older SCSI disks, and it never hurts (although it can be time-consuming). Properly working disks in most modern systems don't require this step, because they have their own internal mechanisms for mapping out bad disk blocks.

Finally, there is a confirmation message because initialization will destroy any data previously on the partition. If all is well, select "Yes." The screen will flash as the initialization program runs.

3.7   Initialize a Linux Partition

At this point, the next menu item presented should be "Initialize a Linux Partition." If it isn't, either you haven't completed the disk partitioning process, or you haven't made one of the menu choices dealing with your swap partition.

You can initialize a Linux partition, or alternately you can mount a previously initialized one. Note that dbootstrap will *not* upgrade an old system without destroying it. If you're upgrading, Debian can usually upgrade itself, and you won't need to use dbootstrap. The Debian 2.1 release notes contain upgrade instructions[2].

If you are using old disk partitions that are not empty, i.e., if you want to just throw away what is on them, you should initialize them (which erases all files). Moreover, you must initialize any partitions that you created in the disk partitioning step. About the only reason to

---

2. http://www.debian.org/releases/slink/i386/release-notes/ch-upgrading.en.html

mount a partition without initializing it at this point would be to mount a partition upon which you have already performed some part of the installation process using this same set of installation floppies.

Select the "Next" menu item to initialize and mount the / disk partition. The first partition that you mount or initialize will be the one mounted as / (pronounced "root"). You will be offered the choice to scan the disk partition for bad blocks, as you were when you initialized the swap partition. It never hurts to scan for bad blocks, but it could take 10 minutes or more to do so if you have a large disk.

Once you've mounted the / partition, the "Next" menu item will be "Install Operating System Kernel and Modules" unless you've already performed some of the installation steps. You can use the arrow keys to select the menu items to initialize or to mount disk partitions if you have any more partitions to set up. If you have created separate partitions for /var, /usr, or other filesystems, you should initialize or mount them now.

3.7.1   Mount a Previously-Initialized Partition

An alternative to the "Initialize a Partition" step is the "Mount a Previously-Initialized Partition" step. Use this if you are resuming an installation that was interrupted or if you want to mount partitions that have already been initialized.

3.8   Install Operating System Kernel and Modules

This should be the next menu step after you've mounted your root partition, unless you've already performed this step in a previous run of dbootstrap. First, you will be asked to confirm that the device you have mounted on root is the proper one. Next, you will be offered a menu of devices from which you can install the kernel. Choose the appropriate device from which to install the kernel and modules; this will either be a CD-ROM device or the first floppy device.

If you're installing from floppies, you'll need to feed in the Rescue Floppy (which is probably already in the drive), followed by the Drivers Floppy.

3.9   Configure PCMCIA Support

There is an alternate step, *before* the "Configure Device Driver Modules" menu selection, called "Configure PCMCIA Support." This menu is used to enable PCMCIA support.

If you do have PCMCIA but are not installing your Debian system using it (i.e., installation with a PCMCIA Ethernet card), you need not configure PCMCIA at this point. You can easily configure and enable PCMCIA at a later point, after installation is complete. However, if you are installing by way of a PCMCIA network device, this alternate must be selected, and PCMCIA support must be configured prior to configuring the network.

If you need to install PCMCIA, select the alternate below "Configure Device Driver Modules." You will be asked which PCMCIA controller your system contains. In most cases, this will be i82365. In some cases, it will be tcic; your laptop's vendor-supplied specifications should provide the information. You can generally leave the next few sets of options blank. Again, certain hardware has special needs; the Linux PCMCIA HOWTO[3] contains plenty of information in case the default doesn't work.

In some unusual cases, you may also need to modify the file /etc/pcmcia/config.opts. You can open your second virtual terminal (Left Alt-F2) and edit the file there and then reconfigure your PCMCIA, or you can manually force a reload of the modules using insmod and rmmod.

Once PCMCIA is properly configured and installed, you should configure your device drivers as described in the next section.

3.10   Configure Device Driver Modules

Select the "Configure Device Driver Modules" menu item and look for devices that are on your system. Configure those device drivers, and they will be loaded whenever your system boots.

You don't have to configure all your devices at this point; what is crucial is that any device configuration required for the installation of the base system is done here.

At any point after the system is installed, you can reconfigure your modules with the modconf program.

---

3. http://metalab.unc.edu/LDP/HOWTO/PCMCIA-HOWTO.html

3.11   Configure the Network

You'll have to configure the network even if you don't have a network, but you'll only have to answer the first two questions – "Choose the Host name," and "Is your system connected to a network?"

If you are connected to a network, you'll need the information you collected from 2.2.1. However, if your primary connection to the network will be PPP, you should choose *NOT* to configure the network.

dbootstrap will ask you a number of questions about your network; fill in the answers from 2.2.1. The system will also summarize your network information and ask you for confirmation. Next, you need to specify the network device that your primary network connection uses. Usually, this will be eth0 (the first Ethernet device). On a laptop, it's more likely that your primary network device is pcmcia.

Here are some technical details you may find handy: The program assumes the network IP address is the bitwise AND of your system's IP address and your netmask. It will guess the broadcast address is the bitwise OR of your system's IP address with the bitwise negation of the netmask. It will guess that your gateway system is also your DNS server. If you can't find any of these answers, use the system's guesses. You can change them once the system has been installed, if necessary, by editing /etc/init.d/network. (On a Debian system, daemons are started by scripts in the directory /etc/init.d/.)

3.12   Install the Base System

During the "Install the Base System" step, you'll be offered a menu of devices from which you may install the base system. Here, you need to select your CD-ROM device.

You will be prompted to specify the path to the base2_1.tgz file. If you have official Debian media, the default value should be correct. Otherwise, enter the path where the base system can be found, relative to the media's mount point. As with the "Install Operating System Kernel and Modules" step, you can either let dbootstrap find the file itself or type in the path at the prompt.

3.12.1   Configure the Base System

At this point you've read in all of the files that make up a minimal Debian system, but you must perform some configuration before the system will run.

You'll be asked to select your time zone. There are many ways to specify your time zone; we suggest you go to the "Directories:" pane and select your country (or continent). That will change the available time zones, so go ahead and select your geographic locality (i.e., country, province, state, or city) in the "Timezones:" pane.

Next, you'll be asked if your system clock is to be set to GMT or local time. Select GMT (i.e., "Yes") if you will only be running Linux on your computer; select local time (i.e., "No") if you will be running another operating system as well as Debian. Unix (and Linux is no exception) generally keeps GMT time on the system clock and converts visible time to the local time zone. This allows the system to keep track of daylight savings time and leap years, and even allows a user who is logged in from another time zone to individually set the time zone used on his or her terminal.

3.12.2 Make Linux Bootable Directly from the Hard Disk

If you elect to make the hard disk boot directly to Linux, you will be asked to install a master boot record. If you aren't using a boot manager (and this is probably the case if you don't know what a boot manager is) and you don't have another different operating system on the same machine, answer "Yes" to this question. Note that if you answer "Yes," you won't be able to boot into DOS normally on your machine, for instance. Be careful. If you answer "Yes," the next question will be whether you want to boot Linux automatically from the hard disk when you turn on your system. This sets Linux to be the *bootable partition* – the one that will be loaded from the hard disk.

Note that multiple operating system booting on a single machine is still something of a black art. This book does not even attempt to document the various boot managers, which vary by architecture and even by sub-architecture. You should see your boot manager's documentation for more information. Remember: When working with the boot manager, you can never be too careful.

The standard i386 boot loader is called "LILO." It is a complex program that offers lots of functionality, including DOS, NT, and OS/2 boot management. To find out more about this functionality, you can read the documentation in **/usr/doc/lilo** after your system is set up.

3.13 Make a Boot Floppy

You should make a boot floppy even if you intend to boot the system from the hard disk. The reason is that it's possible for the hard disk bootstrap to be mis-installed, but a boot floppy will almost always work. Select "Make a Boot Floppy" from the menu and feed the system a blank floppy as directed. Make sure the floppy isn't write-protected, because the software will format and write it. Mark this the "Custom Boot" floppy and write-protect it once it has been written.

3.14 The Moment of Truth

You system's first boot on its own power is what electrical engineers call the "smoke test." If you have any floppies in your floppy drive, remove them. Select the "Reboot the System" menu item.

If are booting directly into Debian and the system doesn't start up, either use your original installation boot media (for instance, the Rescue Floppy) or insert the Custom Boot floppy if you created one, and then reset your system. If you are *not* using the Custom Boot floppy, you will probably need to add some boot arguments. If booting with the Rescue Floppy or similar technique, you need to specify `rescue root=rootfs`, where `rootfs` is your root partition, such as `/dev/sda1`.

Debian should boot, and you should see the same messages as when you first booted the installation system, followed by some new messages.

3.15 Set the Root Password

The *root* account is also called the *superuser*; it is a login that bypasses all security protection on your system. The root account should be used only to perform system administration and for as short a time as possible.

Any password you create should contain from six to eight characters, and it should contain both uppercase and lowercase characters, as well as punctuation characters. Take extra care when setting your root password, since it is such a powerful account. Avoid dictionary words or use of any personal information that could be guessed.

If anyone ever tells you he needs your root password, be extremely wary. You should normally never give out your root account, unless you are administering a machine with more than one system administrator.

3.16 Create an Ordinary User

The system will ask you to create an ordinary user account. This account should be your main personal login. You should *not* use the root account for daily use or as your personal login.

Why not? It's a lot harder to do damage to the system as an ordinary user than as root; system files are protected. Another reason is that you might be tricked into running a *Trojan horse* program – that is, a program that takes advantage of your superuser powers to compromise the security of your system behind your back. Any good book on Unix system administration will cover this topic in more detail. Consider reading one if this topic is new to you.

Name the user account anything you like. If your name is John Smith, you might use "smith," "john," "jsmith," or "js."

3.17   Shadow Password Support

Next, the system will ask whether you want to enable shadow passwords. This is an authentication system that makes your Linux system a bit more secure. Therefore, we recommend that you enable shadow passwords. Reconfiguration of the shadow password system can also be done later with the `shadowconfig` program.

3.18   Remove PCMCIA

If you have no use for PCMCIA, you can choose to remove it at this point. This will make your startup cleaner; also, it will make it easier to replace your kernel (PCMCIA requires a lot of correlation between the version of the PCMCIA drivers, the kernel modules, and the kernel itself). In general, you will not need PCMCIA unless you're using a laptop.

3.19   Select and Install Profiles

The system will now ask you if you want to use the pre-rolled software configurations offered by Debian. You can always choose package-by-package what you want to install on your new machine. This is the purpose of the `dselect` program, described below. But this can be a long task with the thousands of packages available in Debian!

So, you have the ability to choose *tasks* or *profiles* instead. A *task* is work you will do with the machine, such as "Perl programming" or "HTML authoring" or "Chinese word processing." You can choose several tasks. A *profile* is a category your machine will be a member of, such as "Network server" or "Personal workstation." Unlike with tasks, you can choose only one profile.

To summarize, if you are in a hurry, choose one profile. If you have more time, choose the Custom profile and select a set of tasks. If you have plenty of time and want very precise control on what is or is not installed, skip this step and use the full power of `dselect`.

Soon, you will enter into `dselect`. If you selected tasks or profiles, remember to skip the "Select" step of `dselect`, because the selections have already been made.

A word of warning about the size of the tasks as they are displayed: The size shown for each task is the sum of the sizes of its packages. If you choose two tasks that share some packages, the actual disk requirement will be less than the sum of the sizes for the two tasks.

Once you've added both logins (root and personal), you'll be dropped into the `dselect` program. `dselect` allows you to select *packages* to be installed on your system. If you have a CD-ROM or hard disk containing the additional Debian packages that you want to install on your system, or if you are connected to the Internet, this will be useful to you right away. Otherwise, you may want to quit `dselect` and start it later after you have transported the Debian package files to your system. You must be the superuser (root) when you run `dselect`. Information on how to use `dselect` is given in section 3.20.

3.20   Package Installation with `dselect`

It is now time to install the software packages of your choice on your Debian system. This is done using Debian's package management tool, `dselect`.

3.20.1   Introduction

This section documents `dselect` for first-time users. It makes no attempt to explain everything, so when you first meet `dselect`, work through the help screens.

`dselect` is used to select which packages you wish to install (there are currently about 2,250 packages in Debian 2.1). It will be run for you during the installation. It is a very powerful and somewhat complex tool. As such, having some knowledge of it beforehand is highly recommended. Careless use of `dselect` can wreak havoc on your system.

`dselect` will step you through the package installation process outlined here:

1. Choose the access method to use.

2. Update list of available packages, if possible.

3. Select the packages you want on your system.

4. Install and upgrade wanted packages.

5. Configure any packages that are unconfigured.

6. Remove unwanted software.

As each step is completed successfully, `dselect` will lead you on to the next. Go through them in order without skipping any steps.

Figure 3.2   dselect Access screen

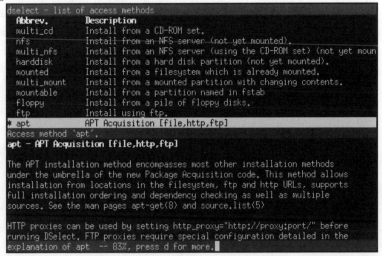

Here and there in this document we talk of starting another shell. Linux has six console sessions or shells available at any one time. You switch between them by pressing Left Alt-F1 through Left Alt-F6, after which you log in on your new shell and go ahead. The console used by the install process is the first one, a.k.a. tty1, so press Left Alt-F1 when you want to return to that process.

3.20.2   Once dselect Is Launched

Once in dselect, you will get this screen:

```
Debian Linux 'dselect' package handling frontend.
0.  [A]ccess  Choose the access method to use.
1.  [U]pdate  Update list of available packages, if possible.
2   [S]elect  Request which packages you want on your system.
3.  [I]nstall Install and upgrade wanted packages.
4.  [C]onfig  Configure any packages that are unconfigured.
5.  [R]emove  Remove unwanted software.
6.  [Q]uit    Quit dselect.
```

Let's look at these one by one.

Access

The Access screen is shown in Figure 3.2 on page 35.

Here we tell dselect where our packages are. Ignore the order that these appear in. It is very important that you select the proper method for installation. You may have a few more methods listed, or a few less, or you may see them listed in a different order; just don't worry about it. In the following list, we describe the different methods.

multi_cd. Quite large and powerful, this complex method is the recommended way of installing a recent version of Debian from a set of multiple binary CDs. Each of these CDs should contain information about the packages in itself and all prior CDs (in the file `Packages.cd`). When you first select this method, be sure the CD-ROM you will be using is not mounted. Place the last *binary* disk of the set (we don't need the source CDs) in the drive and answer the questions you are asked:

```
CD-ROM drive location
Confirmation that you are using a multi-cd set
The location of the Debian distribution on the disk(s)
[ Possibly ] the location(s) of the Packages file(s)
```

Once you have updated the available list and selected the packages to be installed, the multi_cd method diverges from normal procedure. You will need to run an "install" step for each of the CDs you have, in turn. Unfortunately, due to the limitations of `dselect`, it will not be able to prompt you for a new disk at each stage; the way to work for each disk is outlined here:

1. Insert the CD in your CD-ROM drive.

2. From the main `dselect` menu, select "Install."

3. Wait until `dpkg` finishes installing from this CD. (It may report installation successful, or possibly installation errors. Don't worry about these until later.)

4. Press `Return` to go back to the main `dselect` menu.

5. Repeat with the next CD in the set.

It may be necessary to run the installation step more than once to cover the order of package installation; some packages installed early may need to have later packages installed before they will configure properly.

Running a "Configure" step is recommended to help fix any packages that may end up in this state.

multi_nfs, multi_mount. These are similar to the multi_cd method and are refinements on the theme of coping with changing media – for example, installing from a multi_cd set exported via NFS from another machine's CD-ROM drive. indexdselect!multi-NFS, multi-mount installation

apt. One of the best options for installation from a local mirror of the Debian archive or from the network. This method uses the "apt"

F7 VARIABLE PIC 9 COMP-3 VALUE 2.

PAGE | SERIAL | —A | IB | COBOL STATEMENT | IDENT.

PAGE | SERIAL | —A | IB | COBOL STATEMENT

COBOL SOURCE PROGRAM CARD

MC-C 61897

```
dd if=file of=/dev/fd0
   bs=1024 conv=sync;
              sync
```

system to do complete dependency analysis and ordering, so it's most likely to install packages in the optimal order.

Configuration of this method is straightforward. You may select any number of different locations, mixing and matching file: URLs (local disks or NFS mounted disks), http: URLs, or ftp: URLs. Note, however, that the HTTP and FTP options do not support local authenticating proxies.

If you have proxy server for either HTTP or FTP (or both), make sure you set the http_proxy and ftp_proxy environment variables, respectively. Set them from your shell before starting dselect by using the following command:

```
# export http_proxy=http://gateway:3128/
# dselect
```

Update

dselect will read the Packages or Packages.gz files from the mirror and create a database on your system of all available packages. This may take a while as it downloads and processes the files.

Select

Hang on to your hat. This is where it all happens. The object of the exercise is to select just which packages you wish to have installed.

Press Enter. If you have a slow machine, be aware that the screen will clear and can remain blank for 15 seconds. So don't start bashing keys at this point.

The first thing that comes up on the screen is page 1 of the Help file. You can get to this help by pressing ? at any point in the "Select" screens, and you can page through the help screens by hitting the . (full stop) key.

Before you dive in, note these points:

- To exit the "Select" screen after all selections are complete, press Enter. This will return you to the main screen if there is no problem with your selection. Otherwise, you will be asked to deal with that problem. When you are happy with any given screen, press Enter to get out.

- Problems are quite normal and are to be expected. If you select package A and that package requires package B to run, dselect will warn you of the problem and will most likely suggest a solution. If package A conflicts with package B (i.e., if they are mutually exclusive), you will be asked to decide between them.

Table 3.1   Special `dselect` keys

Key	Description
+	Select a package for installation.
=	Place a package on hold
-	Remove a package.
_	Remove a package and its configuration files.
i, I	Toggle/cycle information displays.
o, O	Cycle through the sort options.
v, V	A terse/verbose toggle.

Table 3.2   `dselect` Package States

Flag	Meaning	Possible values
E	Error	Space, R, I
I	Installed State	Space, *, -, U, C, I
O	Old Mark	*, -, =, _, n
M	Mark	*, -, =, _, n

Let's look at the top two lines of the Select screen. This header reminds us of some of the special keys listed in Table 3.1.

Table 3.2 lists the states that `dselect` uses to denote the status of each package it is aware of.

Rather than spell all this out here, I refer you to the Help screens where all is revealed. One example, though.

You enter `dselect` and find a line like this:

```
EIOM Pri  Section  Package   Description
 ** Opt   misc     loadlin   a loader (running under DOS) for LINUX
```

This is saying that `loadlin` was selected when you last ran `dselect` and that it is still selected, but it is not installed. Why not? The answer must be that the `loadlin` package is not physically available. It is missing from your mirror.

The information that `dselect` uses to get all the right packages installed is buried in the packages themselves. Nothing in this world is perfect, and it does sometimes happen that the dependencies built into a package are incorrect, which means that `dselect` simply cannot resolve the situation. A way out is provided where the user can regain control; it takes the form of the commands Q and X, which are available in the Select screen.

QAn override. Forces `dselect` to ignore the built-in dependencies and to do what you have specified. The results, of course, will be on your own head.

XUse X if you get totally lost. It puts things back the way they were and exits.

Select screen (dselect) Keys that help you *not* to get lost (!) are R, U, and
D.

RCancels all selections at this level. Does not affect selections made at the
previous level.

UIf dselect has proposed changes and you have made further changes U
will restore dselect's selections.

DRemoves the selections made by dselect, leaving only yours.

An example follows. The boot-floppies package (not an example for
beginners, I know, but it was chosen because it has a lot of dependencies)
depends on these packages:

- libc6-pic
- slang1-pic
- sysutils
- makedev
- newt0.25
- newt0.25-dev
- popt
- zlib1g
- zlib1g-dev
- recode

The person maintaining boot-floppies also thinks that the following
packages should be installed. These are not, however, essential:

- lynx
- debiandoc-sgml
- unzip

When you select boot-floppies, dselect brings up the conflict resolution
screen. You'll notice that all the required packages have been selected.
Pressing the R key puts things back to the starting point.

```
EIOM Pri Section  Package      Description
  __ Opt admin     boot-floppie Scripts to create the Debian
  __ Opt devel     newt0.25-dev Developer's toolkit for newt
  __ Opt devel     slang1-dev   The S-Lang programming library
  __ Opt devel     slang1-pic   The S-Lang programming library
```

If you decide now that you don't want boot-floppies, just press Enter.
Pressing the D key puts things the way I selected them in the first
place:

```
EIOM Pri Section  Package      Description
  _* Opt admin     boot-floppie Scripts to create the Debian
```

Table 3.3   Expected Package Category States

Package category	Status
Required	all selected
Important	all selected
Standard	mostly selected
Optional	mostly deselected
Extra	mostly deselected

```
__ Opt devel    newt0.25-dev Developer's toolkit for newt
__ Opt devel    slang1-dev   The S-Lang programming library
__ Opt devel    slang1-pic   The S-Lang programming library
```

Pressing the U key restores `dselect`'s selections:

```
EIOM Pri Section Package      Description
_* Opt admin     boot-floppie Scripts to create the Debian installation
_* Opt devel     newt0.25-dev Developer's toolkit for newt
_* Opt devel     slang1-dev   The S-Lang programming library
_* Opt devel     slang1-pic   The S-Lang programming library
```

I suggest running with the defaults for now; you will have ample opportunities to add more later.

Whatever you decide, press Enter to accept and return to the main screen. If this results in unresolved problems, you will be bounced right back to another problem resolution screen.

The R, U, and D keys are very useful in "what if" situations. You can experiment at will and then restore everything and start again. *Don't* look on them as being in a glass box labeled "Break in Case of Emergency."

After making your selections in the Select screen, press I to give you a big window, press t to take you to the beginning, and then use the **Page Down** key to look quickly through the settings. This way you can check the results of your work and spot glaring errors. Some people have deselected whole groups of packages by mistake and not noticed the error until too late. dselect is a *very* powerful tool; don't misuse it.

You should now have the situation shown in Table 3.3.

Happy? Press Enter to exit the Select process. You can come back and run Select again if you wish.

Install

dselect runs through the entire set of packages and installs those selected. Expect to be asked to make decisions as you go. It is often useful to switch to a different shell to compare, say, an old configuration with a new one. If the old file is conf.modules, the new one will be conf.modules.dpkg-dist.

The screen scrolls past fairly quickly on a fast machine. You can stop and start it with Ctrl-s and Ctrl-q, respectively, and at the end of the run, you will get a list of any uninstalled packages.

It can happen that a package does not get installed because it depends on some other package that is listed for installation but is not yet installed. The answer here is to run Install again. Cases have been reported where it was necessary to run it four times before everything slipped into place. This will vary by your acquisition method.

Configure

Most packages get configured in step 3, but anything left hanging can be configured here.

Remove

Removes packages that are installed but no longer required.

Quit

I suggest running /etc/cron.daily/find at this point, because you have a lot of new files on your system. Then you can use locate to get the location of any given file.

3.20.3   A Few Hints in Conclusion

When the install process runs dselect for you, you will doubtless be eager to get Debian running as soon as possible. Well, please be prepared to take an hour or so to learn your way around and then get it right. When you enter the Select screen for the first time, don't make *any* selections at all – just press Enter and see what dependency problems there are. Try fixing them. If you find yourself back at the main screen, run Select again.

You can get an idea of the size of a package by pressing i twice and looking for the "Size" figure. This is the size of the compressed package, so the uncompressed files will be a lot bigger (see "Installed-Size," which is in kilobytes, to know it).

Installing a new Debian system is a complex thing, but dselect can do it for you as easy as can be. So take the time to learn how to drive it. Read the help screens and experiment with i, I, o, and O. Use the R key. It's all there, but it's up to you to use it effectively.

3.21   Glossary

The following terms will be useful to you throughout this book and in general when you're talking about Debian.

Package.A file that contains everything needed to install, de-install, and run a particular program. The program that handles packages is dpkg. dselect is a front-end to dpkg. Experienced users often use dpkg to install or remove a package.

Package names. All package names have the form xxxxxxxxxx.deb. Sample package names include the following:

- efax_08a-1.deb
- lrzsz_0.12b-1.deb
- mgetty_0.99.2-6.deb
- minicom_1.75-1.deb
- term_2.3.5-5.deb
- uucp_1.06.1-2.deb
- uutraf_1.1-1.deb
- xringd_1.10-2.deb
- xtel_3.1-2.deb

4

Logging In

Your system is now installed! Pat yourself on the back for a job well done! Now it's time to start using the system. In this chapter, we introduce you to the Debian command line, some security principles, and how to exit the system. In later chapters, we'll go into more detail on these topics and introduce you to the Debian graphical interface, X11.

4.1 First Steps

After you quit dselect, you'll be presented with the login: prompt. You can now log in using the personal login and password you selected; your system is now ready to use. Let's examine what it means to log in and how this process works.

To use Debian, you must identify yourself to the system. This is so it knows who you are, what you have permission to do, and what your preferences are.

To this end, you have a *username* or *login*. If you installed Debian yourself, you should have been asked to give such a name during installation. If you are logging on to a system administered by someone else, you'll have to ask him for an account on the system and a corresponding username.

You also have a password, so no one else can pretend to be you. If you don't have a password, anyone can log on to your computer from the Internet and do bad things. If you're worried about security, you should have a password.

Many people prefer to trust others not to do anything malicious with their account; hopefully your work environment doesn't encourage paranoia. This is a perfectly reasonable attitude; it depends on your personal priorities and your environment. Obviously a home system does not need to be as secure as a military installation. Debian allows you to be as secure or as insecure as you like.

When you start Debian, you'll see a *prompt*: a request from the computer for some information. In this case, the prompt is `login:`.

You should type your username and, when requested, your password. The password does not appear on the screen as you type it. Press `Enter` after both the username and the password. If you type your username or password incorrectly, you'll have to start over.

If you do it correctly, you'll see a brief message and then a $ prompt. The $ is printed by a special program called the *shell* and is thus called a *shell prompt*. This is where you give commands to the system.

Try entering the command `whoami` now. There is a *cursor* to the right of the shell prompt. Your cursor is a small underscore or rectangle that indicates where you're typing; it should move as you type. Always press `Enter` when you're done typing a shell command.

`whoami` tells your username. You'll then get a new shell prompt.

For the rest of the book, when we say to enter a command, you should type it at the shell prompt and press the `Enter` key.

When you're done working, you may want to log out of the system. To exit the shell, enter the `exit` command. Keep in mind that if you remain logged in, someone could come along and use your account. Hopefully you can trust those in your office or home not to do this; but if you do not trust your environment, you should be certain to log out when you leave.

4.2   Command History and Editing the Command Line

Whatever you type after the shell prompt and before pressing `Enter` is called a *command line*. It's a line of text that commands the computer to do something. The Debian default shell offers several features to make entering command lines easy.

You can scroll up to previous commands to run them again, or you can modify them slightly and *then* run them again. Try this: Enter any command, such as whoami; then press the Up Arrow key. The whoami command will reappear at the prompt. You can then press Enter to run whoami a second time.

If you've entered several commands, you can keep pressing the Up Arrow key to go back through them. This feature is handy if you're doing the same thing several times, or if you type a command incorrectly and want to go back to fix it. You can press the Down Arrow key to move in the other direction, toward your more recent commands. If there are no more commands to move to, the computer will beep.

You can also move around on the command line to make changes. The easiest way is with the Left and Right Arrow keys. Try typing whoasmi instead of whoami, and then use the Left Arrow key to move back to the s. You can erase the s with the Backspace or Delete keys.

There are more advanced features as well (no need to memorize them all now, though). Try pressing Ctrl-a. This moves you to the beginning of the line. Ctrl-k (the k stands for "kill") deletes all characters until the end of the line; try it from the middle of the command line. Using Ctrl-a followed by Ctrl-k, you can delete the entire command line. Ctrl-y pastes the last thing you killed, reinserting it at the current cursor position (y stands for "yank," as in "yank it back"). Ctrl-e will move the cursor to the end of the command line.

Go ahead and play around with command-line editing to get a feel for it. Experiment.

4.3   Working as Root

Because Debian is a multiuser system, it's designed to keep any one user or program from breaking the entire system. The kernel will not allow normal users to change important system files. This means that things stay the way they're supposed to, safe from accidents, viruses, and even malicious pranks. Unlike other operating systems, Debian is safe from these threats. You won't need an anti-virus program.

However, sometimes you need to change important system files; for example, you might want to install new software or configure your network connection. To do so, you have to have greater powers than a normal user; you must become the *root user* (also called the *superuser*).

To become root, just log on with the username root and the root password; this was set during installation, as described in section 3.15 on page 32.

At many sites, only the system administrator has the root password, and only the system administrator can do the things that one must be root to do. If you're using your own personal computer, *you* are the system administrator, of course. If you don't have root privileges, you will have to rely on your system administrator to perform any tasks that require root privileges.

Sometimes you'll have the root password even on a shared corporate or educational server, because the system administrator trusts you to use it properly. In that case, you'll be able to help administer the system and customize it for your needs. But you should be sure to use the password responsibly, respecting other users at all times.

If you have the password, try logging on as root now. Enter the `whoami` command to verify your identity. Then *log out immediately.* When you're root, the kernel will not protect you from yourself, because root has permission to do anything at all to the system. Don't experiment while you're root. In fact, don't do anything as root unless absolutely necessary. This isn't a matter of security, but rather of stability. Your system will run much better if it can keep you from making mistakes.

You may find the `su` command more convenient than logging in as root. su allows you to assume the identity of another user, usually root unless you specify someone else. (You can remember that su stands for Super User, though some say it stands for Set UserID.)

Here's something to try. Log on as yourself – that is, not as root. Then your session will look something like the one in Figure 4.1.

When you're doing system administration tasks, you should do as much as possible as yourself. Then use `su`, do the part that requires root privileges, and use the `exit` command to turn off privileges so you can no longer harm anything.

You can use `su` to assume the identity of any user on the system, not just root. To do this, type `su user` where *user* is the user you want to become. You'll have to know the user's password, of course, unless you're root at the time or the user has no password.

4.4 Virtual Consoles

The Linux kernel supports *virtual consoles.* These provide a way of making your single screen and keyboard seem like multiple terminals that are connected to the same system. Thankfully, using virtual consoles is one of the simplest things about Debian: There are "hot keys" for switching among the consoles quickly. To try it, log in to your system and press `Alt-F2` (simultaneously press the left `Alt` key, and `F2`, that is, function key number 2).

Figure 4.1   Sample session with `su`

```
$ whoami              Check your current username
username              This will show your username
$ su                  Ask system for superuser access
Password:             Type your root password here
machine:~# whoami
root                  You're now on as root
machine:~# exit       Exit your root shell
$ exit                Exit your "normal" shell
```

You should find yourself at another login prompt. Don't panic: You are now on virtual console (VC) number 2! Log in here and do some things – more `whoami` commands or whatever – to confirm that this is a real login shell. Now you can return to virtual console number 1 by pressing `Alt-F1`. Or you can move on to a *third* virtual console, in the obvious way (`Alt-F3`).

Debian comes with six virtual consoles enabled by default, which you access with the `Alt` key and function keys `F1` through `F6`. (Technically, there are more virtual consoles enabled, but only six of them allow you to log in. The others are used for the X Window system or other special purposes.)

If you're using the X Window system, it will generally start up on the first unused virtual console – probably VC 7. Also, to switch from the X virtual console to one of the first six, you'll have to add `Ctrl` to the key sequence. So that's `Ctrl-Alt-F1` to get to VC 1. But you can go from a text VC to the X virtual console using only `Alt`. If you never leave X, you won't have to worry about this; X automatically switches you to its virtual console when it starts up.

Once you get used to them, virtual consoles will probably become an indispensable tool for getting many things done at once. (The X Window system serves much the same purpose, providing multiple windows rather than multiple consoles.) You can run a different program on each VC or log on as root on one VC and as yourself on another. Or everyone in the family can use his or her own VC; this is especially handy if you use X, in which case you can run several X sessions at once on different virtual consoles.

4.5   Shutting Down

Do not just turn off the computer! You risk losing valuable data!

If you are the only user of your computer, you might want to turn the computer off when you're done with it.

To avoid possibly weakening some hardware components, only turn off the computer when you're done for the day. Power up and power down are the two greatest contributors to wear and tear on computer components. Turning the computer on and off once a day is probably the best compromise between your electric bill and your computer's lifespan.

It's a bad thing to just press the power switch when you're done using the computer. It is also bad to reboot the machine (with the Reset button) without first taking proper precautions. The Linux kernel, in order to improve performance, has a *disk cache*. This means it temporarily stores information meant for permanent storage in RAM. Because memory is thousands of times faster than a disk, this makes many file operations move more quickly. Periodically, the information Linux has in memory is actually written to the disk. This is called *syncing*. In order to turn off or reboot the computer safely, you'll have to tell the computer to clear everything out of memory and put it in permanent storage.

To reboot, just type `reboot` or press `Ctrl-Alt-Del` (that's `Ctrl`, `Alt`, and `Delete`).

To shut down, you'll have to log in as `root`. As root, just type the command `shutdown -h now`. The sytem will go through the entire shutdown procedure, including the `sync` command, which clears the disk cache as described above. When you see `System halted`, it's safe to turn off the computer. If you have Advanced Power Management (APM) support in your kernel and BIOS, the computer might shut itself off and save you the trouble. APM is common in laptops and is also found in certain desktop mainboards.

5

The Basics

It's now time to explore the system in more detail. You've seen how to log in and shut down the system. In this chapter, we explore the Linux comand line, how Linux deals with files and directories, and some basics on identifying yourself to others.

5.1 The Command Line and Man Pages

We've already discussed the command line – that is, commands you type after the shell prompt. This section describes the structure of more complicated command lines.

A minimal command line contains just a command name, such as whoami. But other things are possible. For example, you might type: man whoami. This command requests the online manual for the whoami program (you may have to press the space bar to scroll through the documentation or press q to quit). A more complicated example is man -k PostScript. This command line has three parts. It begins with the command name, man. Then it has an *option* or *switch*, -k, followed by an *argument*, PostScript. Some people refer to everything except the command name as the *parameters* of the command. So, options and arguments are both parameters.

Options change the behavior of a command, switching on particular features or functionality. They usually have a - before them. The GNU utilities also have "long forms" for the options; the long form of -k is --apropos. You can enter man -h or man --help to get a full list of options for the man command. Every command will have its own set of options, though most have --help and --version options. Some commands, such as tar, do not require the "-" before their options for historical reasons.

Anything that isn't an option and isn't the command name is an *argument* (in this case, PostScript). Arguments can serve many purposes; most commonly, they are filenames that the command should operate on. In this case, PostScript is the word you want man to search for. In the case of man whoami, the argument was the command you wanted information about.

Here's a breakdown of the man -k PostScript command line:

man. The command name, tells the computer to look at the manual pages. These provide documentation for commands. For example, man whoami will give you documentation on the whoami command.

-k. The option, changes the behavior of man. Normally man expects a command name, such as whoami, for an argument and looks for documentation of that command. But with the -k or --apropos option, it expects the argument to be a keyword. It then gives a list of all manual pages with that keyword in their description.

PostScript. is the argument; because we used the -k option, it's the keyword to search for.

-k and PostScript are both parameters.

Go ahead and type man -k PostScript, and you will see a list of all the manual pages on your system that have something to do with PostScript. If you haven't installed much software, you might see the message PostScript: nothing appropriate instead.

5.1.1 Describing the Command Line

Note: You can skip this section if you want to move on.

There's a traditional, concise way of describing command *syntax*. *Syntax* means the correct ways to combine various options and arguments. For example, if you type man man to get the manual page about man, you'll see several syntax descriptions beginning with the command name man. One of them will look like this: man -k [-M path] keyword ...

Anything in brackets ([]) is an optional unit. In this case you don't have to use the -M option, but if you do, you must use a `path` argument. You must use the -k option and the `keyword` argument. The ... means that you could have more of whatever came before it, so you could look up several keywords.

Let's look at one of the more complex descriptions from the `man` manual page:

```
man [-c|-w|-tZT device] [-adhu7V]
[-m system[,...]] [-L locale] [-p string]
[-M path] [-P pager] [-r prompt] [-S list]
[-e extension] [[section] page ...] ...
```

There's no need to go through all of this (and don't worry about what it all means), but do pay attention to the organization of the description.

First, clusters of options usually mean you can use one or more of them in different combinations, so -**adhu7V** means you can also use -**h**. However, you can't always use all combinations; this description doesn't make that clear. For example, -**h** is incompatible with other options, but you could do `man` -**du**. Unfortunately, the description's format does not make this clear.

Second, the | symbol means "or." So you can use the -c, the -w, *or* the -tZT option, followed by a `device` argument.

Third, notice that you can nest the brackets, because they indicate optional *units*. So if you have a `section`, you must also have a `page`, because e `page` is not optional within the [[section] page] unit.

There's no need to memorize any of this, just refer to this section as you read documentation.

5.2   Files and Directories

Files are a facility for storing and organizing information, analogous to paper documents. They're organized into *directories*, which are called *folders* on some other systems. Let's look at the organization of files on a Debian system:

/. A simple / represents the root directory. All other files and directories are contained in the root directory. If you are coming from the DOS/Windows world, / is very similar to what C:is for DOS, that is the root of the filesystem. A notable difference between DOS and Linux however, is that DOS keeps several filesystems: C: (first hard disk), A: (first floppy disk), and D: (either CD-ROM or second hard disk), whereas Linux has all its files organized above the same / root.

/home/janeq. This is the home directory of user "janeq." Reading left to right, to get to this directory you start in the root directory, enter directory **home**, and then enter directory **janeq**.

/etc/X11/XF86Config. This is the configuration file for the X Window system. It resides in the **X11** subdirectory of the /etc directory. /etc is in turn a subdirectory of the root directory, /.

Things to note:

- Filenames are case-sensitive. That is, **MYFILE** and **MyFile** are *different* files.

- The root directory is referred to as simply /. Don't confuse this "root" with the root user, the user on your system with "super powers."

- Every directory has a name, which can contain any letters or symbols *except* /. The root directory is an exception; its name is / (pronounced "slash" or "the root directory"), and it cannot be renamed.

- While you *can* use almost any letters or symbols in a filename, in practice it's a bad idea. It is better to avoid characters that often have special meanings on the command line, including: { } ( ) [ ] ' ' " \/ > < | ; ! # & ^ * %

- Also avoid putting spaces in filenames. If you want to separate words in a name, good choices are the period, hyphen, and underscore. You could also capitalize each word, **LikeThis**.

- Each file or directory is designated by a *fully-qualified filename*, *absolute filename*, or *path*, giving the sequence of directories which must be passed through to reach it. The three terms are synonymous. All absolute filenames begin with the / directory, and there's a / before each directory or file in the filename. The first / is the name of a directory, but the others are simply separators to distinguish the parts of the filename.

- The words used here can be confusing. Take the following example: /usr/share/keytables/us.map.gz. This is a fully-qualified filename; some people call it a *path*. However, people will also refer to us.map.gz alone as a filename.

- There is also another use for the word "path." The intended meaning is usually clear from the context.

- Directories are arranged in a tree structure. All absolute filenames start with the root directory. The root directory has a number of branches, such as /etc and /usr. These subdirectories in turn branch into still more subdirectories, such as /etc/init.d and /usr/local. The whole thing together is called the "directory tree."

- You can think of an absolute filename as a route from the base of the tree (/) to the end of some branch (a file). You'll also hear people talk about the directory tree as if it were a *family* tree: Thus subdirectories have "parent," and a path shows the complete ancestry of a file.

- There are also relative paths that begin somewhere other than the root directory. More on this later.

- No directory corresponds to a physical device, such as your hard disk. This differs from DOS and Windows, in which all paths begin with a device name such as C:\. The directory tree is meant to be an abstraction of the physical hardware, so you can use the system without knowing what the hardware is. All your files could be on one disk – or you could have 20 disks, some of them connected to a different computer elsewhere on the network. You can't tell just by looking at the directory tree, and nearly all commands work just the same way no matter what physical device(s) your files are really on.

Don't worry if all this isn't completely clear yet. There are many examples to come.

5.2.1   Using Files: A Tutorial

To use your system, you'll have to know how to create, move, rename, and delete files and directories. This section describes how to do so with the standard Debian commands.

The best way to learn is to try things. As long as you aren't root (and haven't yet created any important personal files), you cannot mess up too seriously. Jump in – type each of these commands at the prompt and press Enter.

    pwd

One directory is always considered the *current working directory* for the shell you're using. You can view this directory with the pwd command, which stands for Print Working Directory. pwd prints the name of the directory you're working in – probably /home/yourname.

    ls

ls stands for "list," as in "list files." When you type ls, the system displays a list of all the files in your current working directory. If you've just installed Debian, your home directory may well be empty. If your working directory is empty, ls produces no output, because there are no files to list.

```
cd /
```

cd means "change directory." In this case, you've asked to change to the root directory.

```
pwd
```

This verifies that you're working in the root directory.

```
ls
```

Lets you see what's in /.

```
cd
```

Typing cd with no arguments selects your home directory – /home/ yourname – as the current working directory. Try pwd to verify this.

Before continuing, you should know that there are actually two different kinds of filenames. Some of them begin with /, the root directory, such as /etc/profile. These are called *absolute* filenames because they refer to the same file no matter what your current directory is. The other kind of filename is *relative.*

Two directory names are used *only* in relative filenames: . and ... The directory . refers to the current directory, and .. is the parent directory. These are "shortcut" directories. They exist in *every* directory. Even the root directory has a parent directory – it's its own parent!

So filenames that include . or .. are *relative*, because their meaning depends on the current directory. If I'm in /usr/bin and type ../etc, I'm referring to /usr/etc. If I'm in /var and type ../etc, I'm referring to /etc. Note that a filename without the root directory at the front implicitly has ./ at the front. So you can type local/bin, or ./local/bin and it means the same thing.

A final handy tip: The tilde ~ is equivalent to your home directory. So typing cd ~ is the same as typing cd with no arguments. Also, you can type things like cd ~/practice/mysubdirectory to change to the directory /home/yourname/practice/mysubdirectory. In a similar way, ~myuser is equivalent to the home directory of the user "myuser," which is probably something like /home/myuser; so ~myuser/docs/debian.ps is equivalent to /home/myuser/doc/debian.ps.

Here are some more file commands to try out, now that you know about relative filenames. cd to your home directory before you begin.

```
mkdir practice
```

In your home directory, make a directory called **practice.** You'll use this directory to try out some other commands. You might type ls to verify that your new directory exists.

```
cd practice
```

Changes the directory to `practice`.

    `mkdir mysubdirectory`

Creates a subdirectory of `practice`.

    `cp /etc/profile .`

`cp` is short for "copy." `/etc/profile` is just a random file on your system, don't worry about what it is for now. We've copied it to . (recall that . just means "the directory I'm in now," or the current working directory). So this creates a copy of `/etc/profile` and puts it in your `practice` directory. Try typing `ls` to verify that there's indeed a file called `profile` in your working directory, alongside the new `mysubdirectory`.

    `more profile`

This lets you view the contents of the file `profile`. `more` is used to view the contents of text files. It's called `more` because it shows one screenful of the file at a time, and you press the space bar to see more. `more` will exit when you get to the end of the file, or when you press q (quit).

    `more /etc/profile`

Verifies that the original looks just like the copy you made.

    `mv profile mysubdirectory`

`mv` stands for "move." You've moved the file `profile` from the current directory into the subdirectory you created earlier.

    `ls`

Verifies that `profile` is no longer in the current directory.

    `ls mysubdirectory`

Verifies that `profile` has moved to `mysubdirectory`.

    `cd mysubdirectory`

Changes to the subdirectory.

    `mv profile myprofile`

Note that unlike some operating systems, there is no difference between moving a file and renaming it. Thus there's no separate `rename` command. Note that the second argument to `mv` can be a directory to move the file or directory into, or it can be a new filename. `cp` works the same way.

As usual, you can type `ls` to see the result of `mv`.

    `mv myprofile ..`

Just as . means "the directory I'm in now," .. means "parent of the current directory," in this case the `practice` directory you created earlier. Use `ls` to verify that that's where `myprofile` is now.

```
cd ..
```

Changes directories to the parent directory – in this case `practice`, where you just put `myprofile`.

```
rm myprofile
```

`rm` means "remove," so this deletes `myprofile`. Be careful! Deleting a file on a GNU/Linux system is *permanent* – there is no undelete. If you `rm` it, it's *gone, forever*. Be careful! To repeat, deleting a file on a GNU/Linux system is *permanent* – there is no undelete. If you `rm` it, it's *gone, forever*.

```
rmdir mysubdirectory
```

`rmdir` is just like `rm`, only it's for directories. Notice that `rmdir` only works on empty directories. If the directory contains files, you must delete those files first, or alternatively you can use `rm -r` in place of `rmdir`.

```
cd ..
```

This moves out of the current directory, and into its parent directory. Now you can type the following:

```
rmdir practice
```

This will delete the last remnants of your practice session.

So now you know how to create, copy, move, rename, and delete files and directories. You also learned some shortcuts, like typing simply `cd` to jump to your home directory, and how `.` and `..` refer to the current directory and its parent, respectively. You should also remember the concept of the *root directory*, or `/`, and the alias `~` for your home directory.

5.2.2   Dot Files and `ls -a`

When you type `ls`, files beginning with a dot are not listed. Traditionally, files that contain configuration information, user preferences, and so on begin with a dot; these are hidden and out of your way while you do your day-to-day work. Sample dot files are `~/.emacs`, `~/.newsrc`, `~/.bashrc`, `~/.xsession`, and `~/.fvwmrc`. These are used by Emacs, news readers, the Bash shell, the X Window system, and the fvwm window manager, respectively. It is conventional to end the dot filename with `rc`, but some programs don't. There are also directories beginning with a dot, such as `~/.gimp` and `~/.netscape`, which store preferences for the Gimp and Netscape.

Sometimes a program will create a dot file automatically; for example, Netscape allows you to edit your preferences with a graphical dialog box and then it saves your choices. Other times you will create them yourself using a text editor; this is the traditional way to do it, but you have to learn the peculiar format of each file – inconvenient at first, but it can give you a lot of power.

To see dot files, you must use the -a option to ls. The long form of -a is --all, if you find that easier to remember. You can also use -A or --almost-all, which displays all dot files except . and ... Remember that . is the current directory, and .. is the parent of the current directory; because these are guaranteed to be in every directory, there is no real reason to list them with ls. You already know they are there.

5.3 Processes

We mentioned before that GNU/Linux is a *multitasking* system. It can do many tasks at once. Each of these tasks is called a *process*. The best way to get a sense of this is to type top at the shell prompt. You'll get a list of processes, sorted according to how much of the computer's processing time they're using. The order will continuously change before your eyes. At the top of the display, there's some information about the system: how many users are logged in, how many total processes there are, how much memory you have and how much you're using.

In the far left column, you'll see the user owning each process. The far right column shows which command invoked the process. You'll probably notice that top itself, invoked by you, is near the top of the list (because anytime top checks on CPU usage, it will be active and using CPU to do the check).

Note that in all the commands ending in "d" – such as kflushd and inetd – the "d" stands for *daemon*.

Daemon originally meant Disks And Extensions MONitor. A daemon is a non-interactive process, that is, it's run by the system and users never have to worry about it. Daemons provide services like Internet connectivity, printing, or e-mail.

Now press u and give top your username when it asks. The u command asks to see only those processes belonging to you; it allows you to ignore all the daemons and whatever other people are doing. You might notice bash, the name of your shell. You'll pretty much always be running bash.

Note that column two of the top display shows you the *PID*, or Process IDentification number. Each process is assigned a unique PID. You can use the PID to control individual processes (more on that later). Another useful trick is to press ? to get a list of top commands.

You may wonder about the difference between a "process" and a "program." In practice, people use the terms interchangeably. Technically, the *program* is the set of instructions written by a programmer and kept on disk. The *process* is the working instantiation of the program kept in memory by Linux. But it's not that important to keep the terms straight.

Much of your interaction with a computer involves controlling processes. You'll want to start them, stop them, and see what they're up to. Your primary tool for this is the *shell*.

5.4   The Shell

The *shell* is a program that allows you to interact with your computer. It's called a shell because it provides an environment for you to work in – sort of a little electronic home for you as you compute. (Think hermit crab.)

The simplest function of the shell is to launch other programs. You type the name of the program you want to run, followed by the arguments you want, and the shell asks the system to run the program for you.

Of course, graphical windowing systems also fill this need. Technically, Windows 95 provides a graphical shell, and the X Window system is another kind of graphical shell. But "shell" is commonly used to mean "command-line shell."

Needless to say, the hackers who work on shells aren't satisfied with simply launching commands. Your shell has a bewildering number of convenient and powerful features if you would like to take advantage of them.

There are countless different shells available; most are based on either the *Bourne shell* or the *C shell*, two of the oldest shells. The original Bourne shell's program name is sh, while csh is the C shell. Bourne shell variants include the Bourne Again Shell from the GNU project (bash, the Debian default), the Korn shell (ksh), and the Z shell (zsh). There is also ash, a traditional implementation of the Bourne shell. The most common C shell variant is tcsh (the t pays tribute to the TENEX and TOPS-20 operating systems, which inspired some of tcsh's improvements over csh).

bash is probably the best choice for new users. It is the default and has all the features you're likely to need. But all the shells have loyal followings; if you want to experiment, install some different shell packages and change your shell with the chsh command. Just type chsh, supply a password when asked, and choose a shell. When you next log in, you'll be using the new shell.

5.5   Managing Processes with bash

Debian is a multitasking system, so you need a way to do more than one thing at once. Graphical environments like X provide a natural way to do this; they allow multiple windows on the screen at any one time. Naturally, bash (or any other shell) provides similar facilities.

Earlier you used top to look at the different processes on the system. Your shell provides some convenient ways to keep track of only those processes you've started from the command line. Each command line starts a *job* (also called a *process group*) to be carried out by the shell. A job can consist of a single process or a set of processes in a *pipeline* (more on pipelines later).

Entering a command line will start a job. Try typing man cp, and the cp manual page will appear on the screen. The shell will go into the background and return when you finish reading the manual page (or you can press q to quit rather than scrolling through the whole thing).

But say you're reading the manual page, and you want to do something else for a minute. No problem. Press Ctrl-z while you're reading to *suspend* the current foreground job and put the shell in the foreground. When you suspend a job, bash will first give you some information on it, followed by a shell prompt. You will see something like this on the screen:

```
NAME cp - copy files SYNOPSIS cp [options] source
--More--
[1]+ Stopped man cp
$
```

Note the last two lines. The next to last is the job information, and then you have a shell prompt.

bash assigns a *job number* to each command line you run from the shell. This allows you to refer to the process easily. In this case, man cp is job number 1, displayed as [1]. The + means that this is the last job you had in the foreground. bash also tells you the current state of the job – Stopped – and the job's command line.

There are many things you can do with jobs. With man cp still suspended, try the following commands:

```
man ls
```

Starts a new job.

```
Ctrl-z
```

Suspends the man ls job; you should see its job information.

```
man mv
```

Starts yet another job.

Ctrl-z

Suspends it.

jobs

Asks bash for a display of current jobs. The result looks like this:

```
{$} jobs
[1] Stopped man cp
[2]- Stopped man ls
[3]+ Stopped man mv
{$}
```

Notice the - and +, denoting respectively the next to last and last foreground jobs.

fg

Places the last foreground job (man mv, the one with the +) in the foreground again. If you press the space bar, the man page will continue scrolling.

Ctrl-z

Re-suspends man mv.

fg %1

You can refer to any job by placing a % in front of its number. If you use fg without specifying a job, the last active one is assumed.

Ctrl-z

Re-suspends man cp.

kill %1

Kills off job 1. bash will report the job information, which will look like this:

```
$ kill %1
[1]- Terminated man cp
$
```

bash is only asking the job to quit, and sometimes a job will not want to do so. If the job doesn't terminate, you can add the -KILL[1] option to kill to stop asking and start demanding. For example:

---

1. Many people use the signal number -9 instead of the signal name -KILL. However, it's technically more portable to use the signal name.

```
$ kill -KILL %1
[1]- Killed man mv
$
```

The -KILL option forcibly and unconditionally kills off the job.

In technical terms, kill simply sends a signal. By default, it sends a signal that requests termination (TERM, or signal 15) but you can also specify a signal, and signal 9 (KILL) is the signal that forces termination. The command name kill is not necessarily appropriate to the signal sent; for example, sending the TSTP (terminal stop) signal suspends the process but allows it to be continued later.

```
top
```

This brings the top display back up. Give the u command in top to see only your processes. Look in the right-hand column for the man ls and man mv commands. man cp won't be there because you killed it. top is showing you the system processes corresponding to your jobs; notice that the PID on the left of the screen does not correspond to the job number.

You may not be able to find your processes because they're off the bottom of the screen; if you're using X (see Chapter 9 on page 85), you can resize the xterm to solve this problem.

Even these simple jobs actually consist of multiple processes, including the man process and the pager more, which handles scrolling one page at a time. You may notice the more processes are also visible in top.

You can probably figure out how to clean up the remaining two jobs. You can either kill them (with the kill command) or foreground each one (with fg) and exit it. Remember that the jobs command gives you a list of existing jobs and their status.

One final note: The documentation for bash is quite good, but it is found in the Info help system rather than the man pages. To read it, type info bash. See section A.1.1 for instructions on using the info program. bash also contains a very good summary of its commands accessible by the help command. help displays a list of available topics; more information about each of them is accessible with the command help topic name. Try typing help cd, for example. This will give you details on the -P and -L arguments recognized by cd.

5.6   A Few bash Features

This section mentions just a few of the most commonly used Bash features; for a more complete discussion see Chapter 6.

5.6.1   Tab Completion

The `bash` shell can guess what filename or command you are trying to
type and automatically finish typing it for you. Just type the beginning
of a command or filename and press `Tab`. If `bash` finds a single unique
completion, it will finish the word and put a space after it. If it finds
multiple possible completions, it will fill out the part all completions have
in common and beep. You can then enter enough of the word to make
it unique and press `Tab` again. If it finds no completions, it will simply
beep.

5.7   Managing Your Identity

Unix-like systems are multiuser, and so you have your own electronic
identity as a user on the system. Type `finger yourusername` to look at
some of the information about you that's publically available. To change
the name and shell listed there, you can use the commands `chfn` and
`chsh`. Only the superuser can change your login (username) and directory.
You'll notice that it says "No plan." A "plan" is just some information
you can make available to others. To create a plan, you put whatever
information you want people to see in a file called `.plan`. To do this
you'll use a text editor; see section 8.2 on page 82. Then `finger` yourself
to see your plan. Others can `finger` you to see your plan and to check
whether you've received new mail or read your mail.

Note that this finger information is available to the entire Internet
by default. If you don't want this, read about configuring `inetd` and
the file `/etc/services`. Eventually the installation manual will describe
this configuration, but for now you might try the man pages or just put
nonsense in for your finger information.

6

Using the Shell

As you have been reading this book, you've been interacting with the shell already. The shell is the program that reads your commands and then does what you ask it to. In this chapter, you explore the shell in greater detail, with a special eye towards customizing the shell to work as you want it to.

6.1 Environment Variables

Every process has an *environment* associated with it. An environment is a collection of *environment variables*. A variable is a changeable value with a fixed name. For example, the name EMAIL could refer to the value joe@nowhere.com. The value can vary; EMAIL could also refer to jane@somewhere.com.

Because your shell is a process like any other, it has an environment. You can view your shell's environment by entering the printenv command. Figure 6.1 on page 64 has some sample output from printenv. On your system, the output will be different but similar.

Figure 6.1 Sample `printenv` output

```
PAGER=less
HOSTNAME=icon
MAILCHECK=60
PS1=$
USER=username
MACHTYPE=i486-pc-linux-gnu
EDITOR=emacs
DISPLAY=:0.0
LOGNAME=username
SHELL=/bin/bash
HOSTTYPE=i486
OSTYPE=linux-gnu
HISTSIZE=150
HOME=/home/username
TERM=xterm-debian
TEXEDIT=jed
PATH=/usr/sbin:/usr/sbin:/usr/local/bin:
/usr/bin:/bin:/usr/bin/X11:/usr/games
_=/usr/bin/printenv
```

Environment variables are one way to configure the system. For example, the `EDITOR` variable lets you select your preferred editor for posting news, writing e-mail, and so on.

Setting environment variables is simple. For practice, try customizing your shell's prompt and your text file viewer with environment variables. First, let's get a bit of background information.

> `man less`

This command lets you view the online manual for the `less` command. In order to show you the text one screenful at a time, `man` invokes a *pager* that shows you a new page of text each time you press the space bar. By default, it uses the pager called `more`.

Go ahead and glance over the man page for `less`, which is an enhanced pager. Scroll to a new page by pressing space; press `q` to quit. `more` will also quit automatically when you reach the end of the man page.

> `export PAGER=less`

After reading about the advantages of `less`, you might want to use it to read man pages. To do this, you set the environment variable `PAGER`.

The command to set an environment variable within `bash` always has this format:

Figure 6.2   Changing the prompt

```
$ echo $PS1
$
$ PS1=hello:
hello:echo My prompt is $PS1
My prompt is hello:
hello:
```

```
export NAME=value
```

export means to move the variable from the shell into the environment. This means that programs other than the shell (for instance, a file viewer) will be able to access it.

```
echo $PAGER
```

This is the easiest way to see the value of a variable. **$PAGER** tells the shell to insert the value of the **PAGER** variable *before* invoking the command. echo echoes back its argument: in this case, it echoes the current **PAGER** value, **less**.

```
man more
```

Displays the **more** manual. This time, **man** should have invoked the **less** pager.

less has lots of features that **more** lacks. For example, you can scroll backward with the b key. You can also move up and down (even sideways) with the arrow keys. **less** won't exit when it reaches the end of the man page; it will wait for you to press q.

You can try out some **less**-specific commands, like b, to verify that they don't work with **more** and that you are indeed using **more**.

```
unset PAGER
```

If you don't want to specify a pager anymore, you can **unset** the variable. **man** will then use **more** by default, just as it did before you set the variable.

```
echo $PAGER
```

Because **PAGER** has been unset, echo won't print anything.

```
PS1=hello:
```

Just for fun, change your shell prompt. $ should now change; see Figure 6.2 for details.

export is not necessary, because you're changing the shell's own behavior. There's no reason to export the variable into the environment for other programs to see. Technically, PS1 is a *shell variable* rather than an environment variable.

If you wanted to, you could **export** the shell variable, transforming it into an environment variable. If you do this, programs you run from the shell can see it.

6.2   Where Commands Reside: The PATH Variable

When you type a command into the shell, it has to find the program on your hard disk before executing it. If the shell had to look all over the disk, it would be very slow; instead, it looks in a list of directories contained in the **PATH** environment variable. This list of directories makes up the shell's *search path*; when you enter a command, it goes through each one in turn looking for the program you asked to run.

You may need to change the **PATH** variable if you install programs yourself in a non-standard location. The value of **PATH** is a colon-separated list of directories. The default value on Debian systems is as follows:

```
/usr/local/bin:/usr/bin:/bin:/usr/bin/X11:/usr/games
```

This value is defined in the file /etc/profile and applies to all users. You can easily change the value, just as you can change any environment variable. If you type the command ls, the shell will first look in /usr/local/bin; ls isn't there, so it will try /usr/bin; when that fails, it will check /bin. There it will discover /bin/ls, stop its search, and execute the program /bin/ls. If /usr/bin/X11/ls existed (it doesn't, but pretend), it would be ignored.

You can see which ls the shell is going to use with the **type** command. **type ls** will give you the answer /bin/ls. Try it yourself.

Try asking where **type** itself resides:

```
$ type type
type is a shell builtin
```

type isn't actually a program; it's a function provided by the shell. However, you use it just like an external program.

There are a number of commands like this; type **man builtins** to read the man page describing them. In general, you don't need to know whether a command is a builtin or a real program; however, builtins will not show up in the output of **ps** or **top** because they aren't separate processes. They're just part of the shell.

6.3 Configuration Files

Many applications on Linux systems allow you to alter how they behave at certain times by altering files containing configuration information. These configuration files may contain application start-up information, run-time settings and application shutdown settings. In general, a configuration filename is based on the name of the application for which it contains settings. Such a naming convention allows you to more readily determine which configuration file contains settings for a given application.

6.3.1 System-Wide Versus User-Specific Configuration

It's important to remember that there are two different kinds of configurations on a Debian system. *System-wide configuration* affects all users. System-wide settings are made in the `/etc` directory, so you generally must be root in order to change system-wide settings. You might configure the way the system connects to the Internet, for example, or have web browsers on the system always start on the company home page. Since you want these settings to apply to all users, you make the changes in `/etc`. Sample configuration files in `/etc` include `/etc/X11/XF86Config`, `/etc/lynx.cfg`, and `/etc/ppp/options`. In fact, nearly all the files in `/etc` are configuration files.

User configuration affects only a single user. Dotfiles are used for user configuration. For example, the file `~/.newsrc` stores a list of which USENET (discussion group) articles you have read and which groups you subscribe to. This allows news readers such as `trn` or GNUS to display unread articles in the groups you're interested in. This information will be different for every user on the system, so each user has his own `.newsrc` file in his home directory.

6.4 Aliases

If you use the same command often, you might get tired of typing it. bash lets you write shorter *aliases* for your commands.

Say you always use the `--almost-all` and `--color=auto` options to `ls`. You quickly get tired of typing `ls --almost-all --color=auto`. So you make an alias:

```
alias myls='ls --almost-all --color=auto'
```

Now you can type `myls` instead of the full command. To see what `myls` really is, run the command **type myls**. To see a list of aliases you've defined, simply type **alias** on a line by itself.

Figure 6.3   Redirecting output

```
$ echo Hello > myfile
$ cat myfile
Hello
$
```

6.5   Controlling Input and Output

Throughout your experiences with Linux, you will most likely find that manipulating application input and output can be a very powerful thing to do. This section describes some of the things that controlling input and output can do for you.

6.5.1   `stdin`, `stdout`, Pipelines, and Redirection

Every process has at least three connections to the outside world. The *standard input* is one source of the process's data; the *standard output* is one place the process sends data; and the *standard error* is a place the process can send error messages. (These are often abbreviated `stdin`, `stdout`, and `stderr`.)

The words "source" and "place" are intentionally vague. These standard input and output locations can be changed by the user; they could be the screen, the keyboard, a file, even a network connection. You can specify which locations to use.

When you run a program from the shell, usually standard input comes from your keyboard, and standard output and error both go to your screen. However, you can ask the shell to change these defaults.

For example, the `echo` command sends it output to standard output, normally the screen. But you can send it to a file instead with the *output redirection operator*, `>`. For example, to put the word "Hello" in the file `myfile`, use this command:

```
echo Hello > myfile
```

Use `cat` or your text file pager (`more` or `less`) to view `myfile`'s contents; see Figure 6.3 on page 68.

You can change the standard input of a command with the *input redirection operator*, `<`. For example, `cat < myfile` will display the contents of `myfile`. This is not useful in practice; for convenience, the `cat` command accepts a filename argument. So you can simply say `cat myfile`, and the effect will be the same. redirection operators

Under the hood, `cat < myfile` means that the shell opens `myfile` and then feeds its contents to the standard input of `cat`. `cat myfile`, without the redirection operator, means that the `cat` command receives one argument (`myfile`) opens the file itself, and then displays the file.

There's a reason for the double functionality, however. For example, you can connect the standard output of one command to the standard input of another. This is called a *pipeline*, and it uses the *pipe operator*[1], `|`.

Perhaps you want to see the GNU General Public License in reverse. To do this, you use the `tac` command (it's `cat`, only backward). Try it out:

```
tac /usr/doc/copyright/GPL
```

Unfortunately, it goes by too quickly to read. So you only get to see a couple of paragraphs. The solution is a pipeline:

```
tac /usr/doc/copyright/GPL | less
```

This takes the standard output of `tac`, which is the GPL in reverse, and sends it to the standard input of `less`.

You can chain as many commands together as you like. Say you have an inexplicable desire to replace every `G` with `Q`. For this you use the command `tr G Q`, like this:

```
tac /usr/doc/copyright/GPL | tr G Q | less
```

You could get the same effect using temporary files and redirection, for example:

```
tac /usr/doc/copyright/GPL > tmpfile
tr G Q < tmpfile > tmpfile2
less < tmpfile2
rm tmpfile tmpfile2
```

Clearly a pipeline is more convenient.

6.6   Filename Expansion

Often you want a command to work with a group of files. *Wildcards* are used to create a *filename expansion pattern*: a series of characters and wildcards that expands to a list of filenames. For example, the pattern `/etc/*` expands to a list of all[2] the files in `/etc`.

`*` is a wildcard that can stand for any series of characters, so the pattern `/etc/*` will expand to a list of all the filenames beginning with `/etc/`.

---

1. Depending on your keyboard, this may either appear as a vertical bar or a broken vertical bar, but it can almost always be found above the backslash (`\`).

2. Actually, files beginning with . are not included in the expansion of `*`.

This filename list is most useful as a set of arguments for a command. For example, the `/etc` directory contains a series of subdirectories called `rc0.d`, `rc1.d`, etc. Normally to view the contents of these, you would type the following:

```
ls /etc/rc0.d /etc/rc1.d /etc/rc2.d /etc/rc3.d
ls /etc/rc4.d /etc/rc5.d /etc/rc6.d /etc/rcS.d
```

This is tedious. Instead, you can use the `?` wildcard as shown here:

```
ls /etc/rc?.d
```

`/etc/rc?.d` expands to a list of filenames that begin with `rc`, followed by any single character, followed by `.d`.

Available wildcards include the following:

`*`Matches any group of 0 or more characters.

`?`Matches exactly one character.

`[...]`If you enclose some characters in brackets, the result is a wildcard that matches those characters. For example, `[abc]` matches either a, or b, or c. If you add a `^` after the first bracket, the sense is reversed; so `[^abc]` matches any character that is not a, b, or c. You can include a range, such as `[a-j]`, which matches anything between a and j. The match is case sensitive, so to allow any letter, you must use `[a-zA-Z]`.

Expansion patterns are simple once you see some concrete examples:

`*.txt`This will give you a list of all filenames that end in `.txt`, since the `*` matches anything at all.

`*.[hc]`This gives a list of filenames that end in either `.h` or `.c`.

`a??`This gives you all three-letter filenames that begin with `a`.

`[^a]??`This gives you all three-letter filenames that do *not begin* with `a`.

`a*`This gives you every filename that starts with `a`, regardless of how many letters it has.

More on Files

In section 5.2 on page 51, we covered moving and renaming files with mv, copying them with cp, removing them with rm, removing directories with rmdir, and creating directories with mkdir. This chapter will cover some more aspects of working with files.

7.1 Permissions

GNU and Unix systems are set up to allow many people to use the same computer, while keeping certain files private or keeping certain people from modifying certain files. You can verify this for yourself. Log in as yourself, i.e. *NOT* as root.

```
whoami
```

This verifies that you are not root. Then enter the following command:

```
rm /etc/resolv.conf
```

You should be told `Permission denied`. `/etc/resolv.conf` is an essential system configuration file; you aren't allowed to change or remove it unless you're root. This keeps you from accidentally messing up the system, and if the computer is a public one (such as at an office or school), it keeps users from messing up the system on purpose.

Now type `ls -l /etc/resolv.conf`.

This will give you output that looks something like this:

```
-rw-r--r-- 1 root root 119 Feb 23 1997 /etc/resolv.conf
```

The `-l` option to `ls` requests all that additional information. The info on the right is easy: The size of the file is 119 bytes; the date the file was last changed is February 23, 1997; and the file's name is `/etc/resolv.conf`. On the left side of the screen, things are a little more complicated.

First, the brief, technical explanation: The `-rw-r--r--` is the *mode* of the file, the 1 is the number of hard links to this file (or the number of files in a directory), and the two `root`s are the user and group owning the file, respectively.

So that was cryptic. Let's go through it slowly.

7.1.1   File Ownership

Every file has two owners: a user and a group. The above case is a little confusing because there's a group called `root` in addition to the `root` user. Groups are just collections of users who are collectively permitted access to some part of the system. A good example is a `games` group. Just to be mean, you might create a group called `games` on your computer and then set up your system so that only people in a `games` group are allowed to play games.

Here's a more practical example. Consider a case in which you're setting up a computer for a school. You might want certain files to be accessible only to teachers, not students, so you put all the teachers in a single group. Then you can tell the system that certain files belong to members of the group `teachers`, and that no one else can access those files.

Let's explore groups on the system. First, you can use the `groups` command at the shell prompt. This will show you a list of the groups to which you belong. Here's an example:

```
$ groups
system-wide configuration!permissions!file
ownershipusername dialout cdrom floppy audio
```

It's likely that you're a member of only one group, which is identical to your username. However, root can add you to other groups. The above example shows a person that is a member of five groups.

```
less /etc/group
```

This file lists the groups that exist on your system. Notice the `root` group (the only member of this group is the root user), and the group that corresponds to your username. There are also groups like `dialout` (users who are allowed to dial out on the modem) and `floppy` (users who can use the floppy drive). However, your system is probably not configured to make use of these groups. It's likely that only root can use the floppy or the modem right now. For details about this file, try reading `man group`.

```
ls -l /home
```

This command shows you that every user's directory is owned by that user and that user's personal group.

> Tip: If you just installed Debian, you may be the only user. You can use the `adduser` command to add more users to the system.

7.1.2   Mode

In addition to being owned by one user and one group, every file and directory also has a mode, which determines who's allowed to read, write, and execute the file (and run it, if it's a program). There are a few other things also determined by the mode, but they're advanced topics so we'll skip them for now.

The mode looks like this in the `ls` output: `-rw-r--r--`. For now, we'll consider nine of these parts: those that control *read*, *write*, and *execute* permissions for the *user* owning the file, the *group* owning the file, and *others* (everyone on the system, sometimes called *world*).

In the mode line, the first "element" gives the file type. The - in this case means it's a regular file. If it was `d`, we'd be looking at a directory. There are also other possibilities too complex to go into here; for details, see section 13.2.2 on page 111.

The remaining nine elements are used to display the file's mode. The basic 9 bits (read, write, and execute for user, group, and other) are displayed as three blocks of `rwx`.

So if all permissions are turned on and this is a regular file, the mode will look like this: `-rwxrwxrwx`. If it was a directory with all permissions turned off for others and full permissions for user and group, it would be `drwxrwx---`.

Table 7.1 describes the meaning of the read, write, and execute permissions for both files and directories.

Directory modes can be a little confusing, so here are some examples of the effects of various combinations:

```
r--
```

Table 7.1 Permissions in Linux

Code	Name	Allows for Files	Allows for Directories
r	read	Examine contents of file	List contents of directory
w	write	Modify file	Add or remove files in directory
x	execute	Run as a command	Access files in directory

The user, group, or other with these permissions may list the contents of the directory, but can do nothing else. The files in the directory can't be read, changed, deleted, or manipulated in any way. The only permitted action is reading the directory itself, that is, seeing what files it contains.

rw-

Write permission has no effect in the absence of execute permission, so this mode behaves just like the above mode.

r-x

This mode permits the files in a directory to be listed and permits access to those files. However, files can't be created or deleted. *Access* means that you can view, change, or execute the files as permitted by the files' own permissions.

--x

Files in this directory can be accessed, but the contents of the directory can't be listed, so you have to know what filename you're looking for in advance (unless you're exceptionally good at guessing). Files can't be created or deleted.

rwx

You can do anything you want with the files in this directory, as long as it's permitted by the permissions on the files themselves.

Directory write permission determines whether you can delete files in a directory. A read-only file can be deleted if you have permission to write to the directory containing it. You can't delete a file from a read-only directory even if you're allowed to make changes to the file.

This also means that if you own a directory you can always delete files from it, even if those files belong to root.

Directory execute permission determines whether you have access to files – and thus whether file permissions come into play. *If* you have execute permissions to a directory, file permissions for that directory become relevant. Otherwise, file permissions just don't matter; you can't access the files anyway.

7.1.3 Permissions in Practice

This section goes through a short example session to demonstrate how permissions are used. To change permissions, we'll use the `chmod` command.

```
cd; touch myfile
```

There are a couple of new tricks here. First, you can use ; to put two commands on one line. You can type the above as:

```
$ cd
$ touch myfile
```

or as:

```
$ cd; touch myfile
```

Either way the same thing will end up happening.

Recall that `cd` by itself returns you to your home directory. `touch` is normally used to change the modification time of the file to the current time. But it has another interesting feature: If the file doesn't exist, `touch` creates the file. So you're using it to create a file to practice with. Use `ls -l` to confirm that the file has been created and notice the permissions mode:

```
$ ls -l
-rw-r--r-- 1 user user 0 Nov 18 22:04 myfile
```

Obviously the time and user/group names will be different when you try it. The size of the file is 0, because `touch` creates an empty file. `-rw-r--r--` is the default permissions mode on Debian.

```
chmod u+x myfile
```

This command means to add (+) execute (x) permissions for the user (u) who owns the file. Use `ls -l` to see the effects.

```
chmod go-r myfile
```

Here you've subtracted (-) read permission (r) from the group (g) owning the file and from everyone else (others, o). Again, use `ls -l` to verify the effects.

```
chmod ugo=rx myfile
```

Here you've set (=) user, group, and other permissions to read and execute. This sets permissions to *exactly* what you've specified and unsets any other permissions. So all `rx` should be set, and all `w` should be unset. Now, no one can write to the file.

```
chmod a-x myfile
```

`a` is a shortcut for `ugo`, or "all." So all the `x` permissions should now be unset.

```
rm myfile
```

With this command, you're removing the file, but without write permissions. `rm` will ask if you're sure by displaying the following message:

```
rm: remove 'myfile', overriding mode 0444?
```

You should respond by typing `y` and pressing `Enter`. This is a feature of `rm`, not a fact of permissions. Permission to delete a file comes from the directory permissions, and you have write permission in the directory. However, `rm` tries to be helpful, figuring that if you didn't want to change the file (and thus remove write permission), you don't want to delete it either, so it asks you.

What was that 0444 business in the question from `rm`? The permissions mode is a twelve-digit binary number, like this: 000100100100. 0444 is this binary number represented as an octal (base 8) number, which is the conventional way to write a mode. So you can type `chmod 444 myfile` instead of `chmod ugo=r myfile`.

7.2   Files Present and Their Locations

Now that you can navigate the directory tree, let's take a guided tour of the files and directories you created when you installed Debian. If you're curious, `cd` to each directory and type `ls` to see its contents. If the listing doesn't fit on the screen, try `ls | less`, where | is the "pipe" character, generally found on the same key with backslash.

/As already mentioned, this is the root directory, which contains every other directory.

/**root**But don't get /confused with /root! /root is the home directory of the root user, or superuser. It's a directory called /root, but it isn't *the* root directory /.

/**home**This is where all normal users – that is, all users except root – have their home directories. Each home directory is named after the user who owns it, for example, /home/jane. If you're using a large system at a school or business, your system administrator may create additional directories to contain home directories:

/home1 and /home2 for example. On some other systems, you'll see an additional level of subdirectories: /home/students/username, /home/staff/username, etc.

Your home directory is where you put all your personal work, e-mail and other documents, and personal configuration preferences. It's your home on the system.

/**bin**This directory contains "binaries," executable files that are essential to the operation of the system. Examples are the shell (bash) and file commands such as cp.

/**sbin**This directory contains "system binaries," utilities that the root user or system administrator might want to use, but that you probably won't want to use in your day-to-day activities.

/**usr**/usr contains most of the files you'll be interested in. It has many subdirectories. /usr/bin and /usr/sbin are pretty much like /bin and /sbin, except that the directories in /usr are not considered "essential to the operation of the system."

While not essential to getting the computer working, /usr does contain the applications you'll use to get real work done. Also in /usr, you'll find the /usr/man, /usr/info, and /usr/doc directories. These contain manual pages, info pages, and other documentation, respectively. And don't forget /usr/games!

/**usr**/**local**The Debian system doesn't install anything in this directory. You should use it if you want to install software that you compile yourself or any software not contained in a Debian package. You can also install software in your home directory if you'll be the only one using it.

/**etc**/etc contains all the system-wide configuration files. Whenever you want to change something that affects all users of your computer – such as how you connect to the Internet or what kind of video card you have – you'll probably have to log on as root and change a file in /etc.

/**tmp**Here you'll find temporary files, most of them created by the system. This directory is generally erased on a regular basis or every time you reboot the system. You can create files here if you want, just be aware that they might get deleted automatically.

/**var**/var contains "variable" files that the system changes automatically. For example, incoming mail is stored here. The system keeps a log of its actions here. There are a number of other automatically generated files here as well. You'll mostly be interested in the contents of /var/log, where you can find error messages that can help you figure out what you're system's up to if something goes wrong.

Clearly there are many more directories on the system – far too many to describe every one.

For changing things, you'll usually want to confine yourself to your home directory and /etc. On a Debian system, there's rarely an occasion to change anything else, because everything else is automatically installed for you.

/etc is used to configure the *system* as a whole. You'll use your own home directory, a subdirectory of /home, for configuring your own preferences and storing your personal data. The idea is that on a day-to-day basis, you confine yourself to /home/*yourname*, so there's no way you can break anything. Occasionally you log in as root to change something in a system-wide directory, but only when it's absolutely necessary. Of course, if you're using Debian at a school or business and someone else is the system administrator, you won't have root access and will be able to change only your home directory and any other directory that you own. This limits what you can do with the system.

7.3   File Compression with gzip

Often it would be nice to make a file smaller – say, to download it faster, or so it takes up less space on your disk. The program to do this is called gzip (GNU zip). Here's how it works:

```
$ cd; cp /etc/profile ./mysamplefile
```

This switches to your home directory and copies an arbitrarily chosen file (/etc/profile) to your current directory, in the process renaming it mysamplefile. This gives you a file to play with when using gzip.

```
$ ls -l
```

Lists the contents of the current directory. Note the size of mysamplefile.

```
$ gzip mysamplefile
```

Compresses mysamplefile.

```
$ ls -l
```

Observe the results of this command: mysamplefile is now called mysamplefile.gz . It's also a good bit smaller.

```
$ gunzip mysamplefile.gz; ls -l
```

This uncompresses the file. Observe that mysamplefile has returned to its original state. Notice that to uncompress, one uses gunzip, not gzip.

```
$ rm mysamplefile
```

Use this command to remove the file, since it was just to practice with.

7.4   Finding Files

There are two different facilities for finding files: `find` and `locate`. `find` searches the actual files in their present state. `locate` searches an index generated by the system every morning at 6:42 a.m. (this is a `cron` job, explained elsewhere in this book). `locate` won't find any files that were created after the index was generated. However, because `locate` searches an index, it's much faster - like using the index of a book rather than looking through the whole thing.

To compare the two ways of finding files, pretend you can't remember where the X configuration file `XF86Config` resides.

```
$ locate XF86Config
```

This should be pretty fast. You'll get a list of filenames that *contain* `XF86Config`, something like this:

```
/etc/X11/XF86Config
/usr/X11R6/lib/X11/XF86Config
/usr/X11R6/lib/X11/XF86Config.eg
/usr/X11R6/man/man5/XF86Config.5x.gz
```

Now try the `find` command:

```
$ find / -name XF86Config
```

You will hear a lot of disk activity, and this will take a lot longer. Results will look something like this:

```
/etc/X11/XF86Config
/usr/X11R6/lib/X11/XF86Config
find: /var/spool/cron/atjobs: Permission denied
find: /var/spool/cron/atspool: Permission denied
find: /var/lib/xdm/authdir: Permission denied
```

Notice that `find` found only files that were named *exactly* `XF86Config`, rather than any files containing that string of letters. Also, `find` actually tried to look in every directory on the system - including some where you didn't have read permissions. That's why you got the `Permission denied` messages.

The syntax is different as well. With `find`, you had to specify what directory to search in, whereas `locate` automatically chose the root directory. And you had to specify a search by name using the `-name` option. You could also have searched for files using many other criteria, such as modification date or owner. To have `find` search for files whose names match `XF86Config`, you'd have to use a wildcard:

```
$ find / -name '*XF86Config*'
```

Like most of the command line tools, `find` accepts wildcards as arguments.

In general, `find` is a more powerful utility, and `locate` is faster for everyday quick searches. The full range of possible searches would take a long time to explain; for more details , type `info find`, which will bring up the very thorough info pages on `find` and `locate`.

7.5   Determining a File's Contents

Debian comes with a utility that can guess at the contents of a file for you. Although it is not 100% accurate, you can use the following command to explore your system:

```
$ file /bin/cp
```

You should see something like this:

```
/bin/cp: ELF 32-bit LSB executable, Intel 386, version 1
```

Skipping the technical parts, this is an executable file for Intel machines.

```
$ file /etc/init.d/boot
```

The preceding command gives this response:

```
/etc/init.d/boot: Bourne shell script text
```

meaning that this is a text file containing a Bourne shell script.

7.6   Using a File Manager

Instead of moving files around by hand, you can use a *file manager*. If you move a lot of files around, a file manager can make your work more efficient. There are text-based file managers, such as GNU Midnight Commander (`mc`), and a number of file managers for the X Window system (for example `gmc` for the X Window version of GNU Midnight Commander).

Describing each of these is outside the scope of this book, but you may want to try them out if the command line doesn't meet your needs.

Working with Text Files

Text files are prevelant on a GNU/Linux system. They hold everything from documentation to configuration files. Fortunately, it's easy to work with them.

8.1 Viewing Text Files

A *text file* is simply a normal file that happens to contain human-readable text. There's nothing special about it otherwise. The other kind of file, a binary file, is meant to be interpreted by the computer.

You can view either kind of file with the `less` file pager if you have it installed (install it if you haven't, it's quite useful). Type `less /etc/profile` to view a sample text file. Notice that you can read the characters even if their meaning is obscure. Type `less /bin/ls` to view a binary file. As you can see, the `ls` program is not meant to be read by humans.

Sometimes, you'll find files that end with `.gz`. These files may be viewed with `zless`; you can run it like so:

```
zless /usr/doc/ae/changelog.Debian.gz
```

> Tip: `zless` is great for viewing documentation, which is often shipped in .gz form.

The difference between the two kinds of files is purely a matter of what they contain, unlike in some other systems (such as DOS and MacOS), which actually treat the files differently.

Text files can contain shell scripts, documentation, copyright notices, or any other human-readable text.

Incidentally, this illustrates the difference between *source code* and *binary executables*. `/bin/ls` is a binary executable you can download from Debian, but you can also download a text file that tells the computer how to create `/bin/ls`. This text file is the source code. Comparing `/bin/ls` to `/etc/profile` illustrates how important source code is if someone wants to understand and modify a piece of software. Free software provides you or your consultants with this all-important source code.

8.2   Text Editors

A *text editor* is a program used to create and change the contents of text files. Most operating systems have a text editor: DOS has `edit`, Windows has `Notepad`, MacOS has `SimpleText`.

Debian provides a large variety of text editors. `vi` and `Emacs` are the classic two, which are probably both the most powerful and the most widely used. Both `vi` and `Emacs` are quite complex and require some practice, but they can make editing text extremely efficient. `Emacs` runs both in a terminal and under the X Window system; `vi` normally runs in a terminal but the `vim` variant has a `-g` option that allows it to work with X. text editors

Simpler editors include `nedit`, `ae`, `jed`, and `xcoral`. `nedit` and `xcoral` provide easy-to-use X Window system graphical interfaces. There are also several `vi` variants. Additionally, you can find and a `GNU Emacs` variant called `XEmacs`.

This book does not cover the use of any particular editor in detail, though we will briefly introduce `ae` since it is small, fast, and can be found even on the Debian rescue disks, so it pays to know a bit about it for usage in a pinch. When you need to do more serious editing, check out vim or `GNU Emacs`. `Emacs` provides an excellent interactive tutorial of its own; to read it, load `Emacs` with the `emacs` command and type `F1 t`. `Emacs` is an excellent choice for new users interested in a general-purpose or programming editor.

8.3   Using ae

You can start **ae** by giving it the name of a file to edit, like so:

```
$ ae filename.txt
```

This will bring up an editor screen. The top part of this screen provides some quick help; the bottom shows the file you're editing. Moving around in this editor is simple; just use the arrow keys. You can save the file by pressing C-x C-s and then exit the editor by pressing C-x C-c. Once you feel comfortable with the editor, you can press C-x C-h to turn off the help. That's it! Knowing this will let you do basic editing. For programming or more detailed editing work, you'll want to investigate other editors as discussed earlier.

9

The X Window System

This chapter describes the X Window system graphical user interface. It assumes that you have already successfully configured X as described in the Installation Manual (again, the install manual is not yet written; for now you will need to use the XFree86 HOWTO, the contents of /usr/doc/X11, and this chapter). Once you install X, you can enter the X environment by typing `startx` or via `xdm`, depending on your choice during configuration.

9.1 Introduction to X

A GUI (Graphical User Interface) is part and parcel of the Windows and Mac operating systems. It's basically impossible to write an application for those systems that does not use the GUI, and the systems can't be used effectively from the command line. GNU/Linux is more *modular*, that is, it's made up of many small, independent components that can be used or not according to one's needs and preferences. One of these components is the X Window system, or simply X.

This component is also sometimes called X11. Please note that "X Windows" is *not* correct.

X itself is a means for programs to talk to your mouse and video card without knowing what kind of mouse and video card you have. That is, it's an *abstraction* of the graphics hardware. User applications talk to X in X's language; X then translates into the language of your particular hardware. This means that programs only have to be written once, and they work on everyone's computer.

In X jargon, the program that speaks to the hardware is known as an *X server*. User applications that ask the X server to show windows or graphics on the screen are called *X clients*. The X server includes a *video driver*, so you must have an X server that matches your video card.

The X server doesn't provide any of the features one might expect from a GUI, such as resizing and rearranging windows. A special X client, called a *window manager*, draws borders and title bars for windows, resizes and arranges windows, and provides facilities for starting other X clients from a menu. Specific window managers may have additional features.

Window managers available on a Debian system include `fvwm`, `fvwm2`, `icewm`, `afterstep`, `olvwm`, `wmaker`, `twm`, and `enlightenment`. You'll probably want to try them all and pick your favorite.

Neither the X server nor the window manager provide a *file manager*; that is, there aren't any windows containing icons for your files and directories. You can launch a file manager as a separate application, and there are many of them available. The GNOME desktop project is developing an icon-based file manager and other GUI facilities. See the GNOME homepage[1] for the latest news on this.

A final feature of X is its *network transparency*, meaning that X clients don't care if they're talking to an X server on the same machine or an X server somewhere on the network. In practical terms, this means you can run a program on a more powerful remote machine but display it on your desktop computer.

9.2   Starting the X Environment

There are two ways to start X. The first is to start X manually when you feel like using it. To do so, log in to one of the text consoles and type `startx`. This will start X and switch you to its virtual console.

The second (and recommended) way to use X is with `xdm` or X Display Manager. Basically, `xdm` gives you a nice graphical login prompt on the X virtual console (probably VC 7), and you log in there.

---

1. http://www.gnome.org/

By default, either method will also start an `xterm`, which is a small window containing a shell prompt. At the shell prompt, you can type any commands just as you would on a text VC. So you can follow all the examples in this book using `xterm`; the only difference between an `xterm` and the text console is that you don't have to log on to the `xterm` because you already logged on to X.

There are also a lot of things you can do only in X, which are covered in this chapter.

One note: The default `xterm` window has a smallish font. If you have a small monitor or very high resolution or bad eyesight, you may want to fix this. Follow these steps:

1. Move the mouse pointer into the center of the `xterm` window.
2. Hold down the `Control` key and the *right* mouse button simultaneously. This will give you a font menu.
3. Point to the font you want and release the mouse button.

9.3   Basic X Operations

There are certain commonly used operations in X that you should familiarize yourself with. This section describes some of the basic operations that you may find useful.

9.3.1   The Mouse

The mouse in X works pretty much the same as the mouse on other systems, except that it has three buttons. If your mouse has only two, you can simulate the middle button by clicking both buttons simultaneously. This is kind of tricky and annoying, so investing in a $15 three-button mouse probably isn't a bad idea. These are available from most computer retailers.

The buttons are numbered from left to right assuming you have a right-handed mouse. So button one is on the left, two is in the middle, and three is on the right. You may see either the numbers or the locations in documentation.

X has a simple built-in copy-and-paste facility. To select text to copy, you click and drag with the left mouse button. This should select the text to copy, assuming the application you're using has copy-and-paste support. To paste the text, you click the middle mouse button in a different X application. For example, if you receive an e-mail containing an URL, you can select the URL with the left button and then click in your web browser's "Location" field with the middle button to paste it in.

9.3.2   X Clients

Programs that communicate with the X server are called X clients. Most of these programs will ask the X server to display windows on the screen.

You start an X client the same way you start any other Debian program. Simply type the name of the client on the command line. Try typing xterm into an existing xterm window, and a new xterm client will appear on the screen.

You may notice that the original xterm is now useless, because your shell is waiting for the second xterm to finish. To avoid this problem, you can run the X client in the backgroundby adding a & after the command name like this: xterm &. If you forget, you can place a running process in the background. First suspend the process with CTRL-z, and then place it in the background with the bg command.

If you use a program often, your window manager will generally provide a way to put that program on a convenient graphical menu.

9.3.3   Troubleshooting

Sometimes when you launch an X client from a graphical menu, you won't be able to see any error messages if it fails. You can find any error messages in the file ~/.xsession-errors.

9.3.4   Leaving the X Environment

To leave X, you need to use a menu. Unfortunately for beginners, this is different for every window manager, and for most window managers, it can be configured in many ways. If there's an obvious menu, look for an entry like "Exit" or "Close Window Manager." If you don't see a menu, try clicking each of the mouse buttons on the background of the screen. If all else fails, you can forcibly kill the X server by pressing CTRL-ALT-Backspace. Forcibly killing the server destroys any unsaved data in open applications.

9.4   Customizing Your X Startup

When you start X, Debian runs some shell scripts that start your window manager and other X clients. By default, a window manager, an xconsole, and an xterm are started for you.

To customize your X startup, the file /etc/X11/config must contain the line allow-user-xsession. If it does not, log in as root and add the line now. Then log back in as yourself and continue the tutorial.

You can see how Debian's X startup works in the file /etc/X11/Xsession. Note that you can change the behavior of /etc/X11/Xsession by modifying the file /etc/X11/config, which specifies a few system-wide preferences.

To run the clients of your choice when X starts, you create an executable shell script called .xsession in your home directory.

```
$ touch ~/.xsession
```

This creates the file.

```
$ chmod u+x ~/.xsession
```

This makes the file executable.

Once .xsession is created, you need to edit it to do something useful with your favorite text editor. You can do anything you want to in this script. However, when the script's process terminates, X also terminates.

In practical terms, this means that you often end the script with a call to exec. Whatever program you exec will replace the script process with itself, so commands found after the exec line will be ignored. The program you exec will become the new owner of the script process, which means that X will terminate when this new program's process terminates.

Say you end your .xsession with the line exec fvwm. This means that the fvwm window manager will be run when X starts. When you quit the fvwm window manager, your X session will end, and all other clients will be shut down. You do not have to use a window manager here; you could exec xterm, in which case typing exit in that particular xterm would cause the entire X session to end.

If you want to run other clients before you use exec, you will need to run them in the background. Otherwise .xsession will pause until each client exits and then continue to the next line. See the previous section on running jobs in the background (basically you want to put an ampersand at the end, as in xterm &).

You can take advantage of this behavior, though. If you want to run commands at the end of your X session, you can have your .xsession run a window manager or the like and wait for it to finish. That is, leave off the exec and the &; just enter fvwm by itself. Then put the commands of your choice after fvwm.

It would probably help to look at a few sample .xsession files. In all the examples, replace fvwm with the window manager of your choice.

The simplest .xsession just runs a window manager:

```
exec fvwm
```

This will run fvwm, and the X session will end when fvwm exits. If you do it without the exec, everything will appear to behave the same way, but behind the scenes .xsession will hang around waiting for fvwm, and .xsession will exit after fvwm does. Using exec is slightly better because fvwm replaces .xsession instead of leaving it waiting. You can use the ps or top command to verify this.

A more useful .xsession runs a few clients before starting the window manager. For example, you might want some xterms and an xclock whenever you start X. No problem; just enter xterm & xterm & xclock & exec fvwm. Two xterms and an xclock start up in the background, and then the window manager is launched. When you quit the window manager, you'll also quit X.

You might try it without the backgrounding just to see what happens. Enter this command: xterm xclock exec fvwm. xterm will start, and wait for you to exit it. Then xclock will start; you'll have to exit xclock before fvwm will start. The commands are run in sequence, since the script waits for each one to exit.

You can use sequential execution to your advantage. Perhaps you want to keep track of when you stop working every day:

```
xterm &
xclock &
fvwm
date >> ~/logout-time
```

This will fork off an xterm and an xclock and then run fvwm and wait for it to finish. When you exit fvwm, it will move on to the last line, which appends the current date and time to the file ~/logout-time.

Finally, you can have a program other than the window manager determine when X exits:

```
xclock &
fvwm &
exec xterm
```

This script will run xclock and fvwm in the background and then replace itself with xterm. When you exit the xterm, your X session will end.

The best way to learn how to use .xsession is to try some of these things out. Again, be sure you use **chmod** to make it executable; failure to do so is a common error.

10

Filesystems

A Debian system uses a filesystem to store and manage your data. This chapter introduces you to the filesystem, describes how to add and remove filesystems, and shows you how to back up your system.

10.1 Concepts

It's probably a good idea to explain a little theory before discussing the mechanics of using disks. In particular, you must understand the concept of a *filesystem*. This can be a bit confusing because it has several meanings.

The filesystem refers to the whole directory tree, starting with the root directory /, as described in earlier chapters.

A filesystem in general means any organization of files and directories on a particular physical device. "Organization" means the hierarchical directory structure and any other information about files one might want to keep track of: their size, who has permission to change them, etc. So you might have one filesystem on your hard disk, and another one on each floppy disk.

"Filesystem" is also used to mean a *type* of filesystem. For example, MS-DOS and Windows 3.1 organize files in a particular way, with particular rules: Filenames can have only eight characters, for example, and no permission information is stored. Linux calls this the `msdos` filesystem. Linux also has its own filesystem, called the `ext2` filesystem (version two of the `ext` filesystem). You'll use the `ext2` filesystem most of the time unless you're accessing files from another operating system or have other special needs.

Any physical device you wish to use for storing files must have at least one filesystem on it. This means a filesystem in the second sense – a hierarchy of files and directories, along with information about them. Of course, any filesystem has a type, so the third sense will come into play as well. If you have more than one filesystem on a single device, each filesystem can have a different type – for example, you might have both a DOS partition and a Linux partition on your hard disk.

10.2   `mount` and `/etc/fstab`

This section describes how to mount a floppy or Zip disk, discusses the `/dev` directory, and addresses distributing the directory tree over multiple physical devices or partitions.

10.2.1   Mounting a Filesystem

On a GNU/Linux system there's no necessary correspondence between directories and physical devices as there is in Windows, in which each drive has its own directory tree beginning with a letter (such as `C:\`).

Instead, each physical device such as a hard disk or floppy disk has one or more filesystems on it. In order to make a filesystem accessible, it's assigned to a particular directory in another filesystem. To avoid circularity, the root filesystem (which contains the root directory /) is not stored within any other filesystem. You have access to it automatically when you boot Debian.

A directory in one filesystem that contains another filesystem is known as a *mount point*. A mount point is a directory in a first filesystem on one device (such as your hard disk) that "contains" a second filesystem, perhaps on another device (such as a floppy disk). To access a filesystem, you must mount it at some mount point.

So, for example, you might mount a CD at the mount point `/cdrom`. This means that if you look in the directory `/cdrom`, you'll see the contents of the CD. The `/cdrom` directory itself is actually on your hard disk. For all practical purposes, the contents of the CD become a part of the root filesystem, and when you type commands and use programs, it doesn't make any difference what the actual physical location of the files is. You could have created a directory on your hard disk called /cdrom and put some files in it, and everything would behave in exactly the same way. Once you mount a filesystem, there's no need to pay any attention to physical devices.

However, before you can mount a filesystem or actually create a filesystem on a disk that doesn't have one yet, it's necessary to refer to the devices themselves. All devices have names, which are located in the /dev directory. If you type ls /dev now, you'll see a pretty lengthy list of every possible device you could have on your Debian system. For a summary of some devices, see Table 2.1 on page 15. A more thorough list can be found on your system in the file /usr/src/linux/Documentation/devices.txt.

To mount a filesystem, we want to tell Linux to associate whatever filesystem it finds on a particular device with a particular mount point. In the process, we might have to tell Linux what kind of filesystem to look for.

10.2.2   Example: Mounting a CD-ROM

As a simple demonstration, we'll go through mounting a CD-ROM, such as the one you may have used to install Debian. You'll need to be root to do this, so be careful; whenever you're root, you have the power to manipulate the whole system, not just your own files. Also, these commands assume there's a CD in your drive; you should put one in the drive now. Then start with the following command:

    su

If you haven't already, you need to either log in as root or gain root privileges with the su (super user) command. If you use su, enter the root password when prompted.

    ls /cdrom

Use this command to see what's in the /cdrom directory before you start. If you don't have a /cdrom directory, you may have to make one using mkdir /cdrom.

    mount

Simply typing mount with no arguments lists the currently mounted filesystems.

    mount -t iso9660 *CD-device* /cdrom

For this command, you should substitute the name of your CD-ROM device for *CD-device* in the above command line. If you aren't sure,

/dev/cdrom is a good guess because the install process should have created this symbolic link on the system. If that fails, try the different IDE devices: /dev/hdc, etc. You should see a message like this: mount: block device /dev/hdc is write-protected, mounting read-only.

The -t option specifies the type of the filesystem, in this case iso9660. Most CDs are iso9660. The next argument is the name of the device to mount, and the final argument is the mount point. There are many other arguments for mount; see the manual page for details.

Once a CD is mounted, you may find that your drive tray will not open. You must unmount the CD before removing it.

    ls /cdrom

Confirms that /cdrom now contains whatever is on the CD in your drive.

    mount

Displays the list of filesystems again; notice that your CD drive is now mounted.

    umount /cdrom

This unmounts the CD. It's now safe to remove the CD from the drive. Notice that the command is umount with no "n," even though it's used to unmount the filesystem.

    exit

Don't leave yourself logged on as root. Log out immediately, just to be safe.

10.2.3   /etc/fstab: Automating the Mount Process

The file /etc/fstab (it stands for "filesystem table") contains descriptions of filesystems that you mount often. These filesystems can then be mounted with a shorter command, such as mount /cdrom. You can also configure filesystems to mount automatically when the system boots. You'll probably want to mount all of your hard disk filesystems when you boot, so Debian automatically adds entries to fstab to do this for you.

Look at this file now by typing more /etc/fstab. It will have two or more entries that were configured automatically when you installed the system. It probably looks something like this:

```
# /etc/fstab: static file system information.
#
# <file system> <mount point> <type> <options>
#<dump > <pass>
/dev/hda1 / ext2 defaults 0 1
/dev/hda3 none swap sw 0 0
```

```
proc /proc proc defaults 0 0
/dev/hda5 /tmp ext2 defaults 0 2
/dev/hda6 /home ext2 defaults 0 2
/dev/hda7 /usr ext2 defaults 0 2
/dev/hdc /cdrom iso9660 ro,noauto 0 0
/dev/fd0 /floppy auto noauto,sync 0 0
```

The first column lists the device the filesystem resides on. The second lists the mount point, the third indicates the filesystem type. The line beginning by `proc` is a special filesystem. Notice that the swap partition (`/dev/hda3` in the example) has no mount point, so the mount point column contains `none`.

The last three columns may require some explanation.

The fifth column is used by the `dump` utility to decide when to back up the filesystem. In most cases, you can put 0 here.

The sixth column is used by `fsck` to decide in what order to check filesystems when you boot the system. The root filesystem should have a 1 in this field, filesystems that don't need to be checked (such as the swap partition) should have a 0, and all other filesystems should have a 2. It's worth noting that the swap partition isn't exactly a filesystem in the sense that it does not contain files and directories but is just used by the Linux kernel as secondary memory. However, for historical reasons, the swap partitions are still listed in the same file as the filesystems.

Column four contains one or more options to use when mounting the filesystem. You can check the `mount` manpage for a summary; see section 5.1 on page 49.

10.2.4   Removable Disks (Floppies, Zip Disks, Etc.)

Add the following lines to your `/etc/fstab` file:

```
/dev/sda1 /mnt/zip ext2 noauto,user 0 0
/dev/sda4 /mnt/dos msdos noauto,user 0 0
```

From now on, you'll be able to mount the DOS-formatted Zip disks with the command `mount /mnt/dos`, and you be able to mount Linux-formatted Zip disks with the command `mount /mnt/zip`.

If you have SCSI hard disks in your system, you'll have to change `sda` to `sdb` or `sdc` in the example above.

10.3   Backup Tools

Backups are important under any operating system. Debian GNU/Linux provides several different utilities that you might want to use. Additionally, while many of these utilities were aimed at tape backups originally, you'll find that they are now being used for other things. For instance, tar is being used for distributing programs over the Internet. Some of the utilities that you'll find include the following:

- Taper is a menu-driven, easy-to-learn backup program that can back up to a variety of media. Its limitation is that it doesn't handle large (4GB or larger) backups.

- dump is designed specifically for tapes; its main strengths are its interface for file restores, low-level filesystem backups, and incremental backup scheduling. Its limitations include the inability to back up NFS or other non-ext2 filesystems and some rather arcane defaults.

- GNU tar (short for Tape ARchiver) is an implementation of what is probably the most widely used backup or archiving utility in Linux today. It makes a good general purpose tool and can deal with the widest variety of target media. Additionally, many different systems can read tar files, making them highly portable. tar's weaknesses include a weaker incremental backup system than dump and no interactive restore selection screen.

10.3.1   tar

Because tar is used so much, and for quite a bit in addition to backups, it is being described here. For more details, see the tar manual page; instructions for viewing manual pages can be found in section 5.1 on page 49.

tar is an *archiver*. This means that tar can take many files and combine them all into one large file or write them out to a backup device such as a tape drive. Once you have this one large file, you will often want to compress it; the -z option is great for this. Hence, tar offers a great way to distribute programs and data on the Internet, and you'll find that it is used extensively for this purpose.

Here's a sample tar command line:

```
tar -zcvf myfiles.tar.gz /usr/local/bin
```

Let's take a look at how this command can be broken down:

tarName of the command.

-Tells tar that options will follow.

zTells tar to use gzip compression automatically; if you use this, it's good to add a .gz extension as well.

cTells tar to create a new archive.

vThis says to be verbose; that is, it tells tar to let you know what it's doing while it creates the archive.

f This indicates that the next thing on the command line is the name of the file to be created or the device to be used. If I used /dev/st0 here, for instance, it would write the backup to the tape drive.

myfiles.tar.gz This is the name of the file to be created.

/usr/local/bin This is the name of the file or directory to store in the archive. It's also possible to specify several items here.

You may often find `tar.gz` files (or simply `tgz` files) on the Internet. You can unpack these with a command like:

```
tar -zxvf filename.tar.gz
```

11

Networking

One of the key benefits of GNU/Linux over other systems lies in its networking support. Few systems can rival the networking features present in GNU/Linux. In this chapter, we tell you how to configure your network devices.

11.1 PPP

This section is a quick-start guide to setting up PPP on Debian. If it turns out that you need more details, see the excellent PPPHOWTO from the Linux Documentation Project. The HOWTO goes into much more detail if you're interested or have unique needs.

11.1.1 Introduction

If you connect to the Internet over a phone line, you'll want to use PPP (Point-to-Point Protocol). This is the standard connection method offered by ISPs (Internet service providers). In addition to using PPP to dial your ISP, you can have your computer listen for incoming connections – this lets you dial your computer from a remote location.

11.1.2   Preparation

Configuring PPP on Debian GNU/Linux is straightforward once you have all the information you'll need. Debian makes things even easier with its simple configuration tools.

Before you start, be sure you have all the information provided by your ISP. This might include:

- Username or login
- Password
- Your static IP (Internet Protocol) address, if any (these look like 209.81.8.242). This information isn't needed for most ISPs.
- Bitmask (this will look something like 255.255.255.248). This information isn't needed for most ISPs.
- The IP addresses of your ISP's name servers (or DNS).
- Any special login procedure required by the ISP.

Next, you'll want to investigate your hardware setup: whether your modem works with GNU/Linux and which serial port it's connected to.

A simple rule determines whether your modem will work. If it's a "winmodem" or "host-based modem," it won't work. These modems are cheap because they have very little functionality, and they require the computer to make up for their shortcomings. Unfortunately, this means they are complex to program, and manufacturers generally do not make the specifications available for developers.

If you have a modem with its own on-board circuitry or an external modem, you should have no trouble at all.

On GNU/Linux systems, the serial ports are referred to as /dev/ttyS0, /dev/ttyS1, and so on. Your modem is almost certainly connected to either port 0 or port 1, equivalent to COM1: and COM2: under Windows. If you don't know which your modem is connected to, run the program wvdialconf to try to detect it (see below); otherwise, just try both and see which works.

If you want to talk to your modem or dial your ISP without using PPP, you can use the minicom program. You may need to install the minicom package to make the program available.

11.1.3   The Easy Way: wvdial

The simplest way to get PPP running is with the wvdial program. It makes some reasonable guesses and tries to set things up for you. If it works, you're in luck. If it guesses wrong, you'll have to do things manually.

Be sure you have the following packages installed:

- ppp
- ppp-pam
- wvdial

When you install the wvdial package, you may be given the opportunity to configure it. Otherwise, to set up wvdial, follow these simple steps:
Log in as root, using su (as described in an earlier chapter).

    touch /etc/wvdial.conf

touch will create the following file if the file doesn't exist; the configuration program requires an existing file.

    wvdialconf /etc/wvdial.conf

This means you're creating a configuration file, /etc/wvdial.conf.

Answer any questions that appear on the screen. wvdialconf will also scan for your modem and tell you which serial port it's on; you may want to make a note of this for future reference.

11.2   Ethernet

Another popular way to connect to the Internet is via a LAN that uses Ethernet. This gives you a high-speed local network in addition to Internet access. Fortunately, though, you should have already configured Ethernet networking during installation so there isn't much you need to do now. If you ever need to modify your configuration, here are the files that you will be interested in:

- /etc/init.d/network has things such as your IP address, netmask, and default route.
- /etc/hostname records your hostname.
- /etc/hosts also records your hostname and IP address.

12

Removing and Installing Software

This chapter describes ways of installing and removing software packages. There are several ways of doing both. Here we discuss installation and removal of pre-built software, such as Debian packages, and installation of source that must be built by you.

12.1 What a Package Maintenance Utility Does

An application or utility program usually involves quite a few files. It might include libraries, data files like game scenarios or icons, configuration files, manual pages, and documentation. When you install the program, you want to make sure you have all the files you need in the right places.

You'd also like to be able to uninstall the program. When you uninstall, you want to be sure all the associated files are deleted. However, if a program you still have on the system needs those files, you want to be sure you keep them.

Finally, you'd like to be able to upgrade a program. When you upgrade, you want to delete obsolete files and add new ones, without breaking any part of the system.

The Debian package system solves these problems. It allows you to install, remove, and upgrade software *packages*, which are neat little bundles containing the program files and information that helps the computer manage them properly. Debian packages have filenames ending in the extension .deb, and they're available on the FTP site or on your official Debian CD-ROM.

12.2   dpkg

The simplest way to install a single package you've downloaded is with the command dpkg -i (short for dpkg --install). Say you've downloaded the package icewm_0.8.12-1.deb and you'd like to install it. First log on as root, and then type dpkg -i icewm_0.8.12-1.deb, and icewm version 0.8.12 will be installed. If you already had an older version, dpkg will upgrade it rather than installing both versions at once.

If you want to remove a package, you have two options. The first is most intuitive: dpkg -r icewm. This will remove the icewm package (-r is short for --remove). Note that you give only the icewm for --remove, whereas --install requires the entire .deb filename.

--remove will leave configuration files for the package on your system. A configuration file is defined as any file you might have edited in order to customize the program for your system or your preferences. This way, if you later reinstall the package, you won't have to set everything up a second time.

However, you might want to erase the configuration files too, so dpkg also provides a --purge option. dpkg --purge icewm will permanently delete every last file associated with the icewm package.

12.3   dselect

dselect is a great front-end for dpkg. dselect provides a menu interface for dpkg, and can automatically fetch the appropriate files from a CD-ROM or Internet FTP site. For details on using dselect, see section 3.20 on page 34.

12.4   Compiling Software

Many programs come in source format, often in tar.gz form. First, you must unpack the tar.gz file; for details on doing this, see section 10.3.1

on page 96. Before you can compile the package, you'll need to have gcc, libc6-dev, and other relevant "-dev" packages installed; most of these are listed in the devel area in dselect.

With the appropriate packages installed, cd into the directory that tar created for you. At this point, you'll need to read the installation instructions. Most programs provide an INSTALL or README file that will tell you how to proceed.

13

Advanced Topics

By now, you should have a strong base for which to build your GNU/Linux skills on. In this chapter we cover some very useful information regarding some advanced GNU/Linux features.

13.1 Regular Expressions

A regular expression is a description of a set of characters. This description can be used to search through a file by looking for text that *matches* the regular expression. Regular expressions are analogous to shell wildcards (see section 6.6 on page 69), but they are both more complicated and more powerful.

A regular expression is made up of text and *metacharacters*. A metacharacter is just a character with a special meaning. Metacharacters include the following: . * [] - \^ $.

If a regular expression contains only text (no metacharacters), it matches that text. For example, the regular expression "my `regular expression`" matches the text "`my regular expression`," and nothing else. Regular expressions are usually case sensitive.

You can use the `egrep` command to display all lines in a file that contain a regular expression. Its syntax is as follows:

```
egrep 'regexp' filename1 ...
```

The single quotation marks are not always needed, but they never hurt.

For example, to find all lines in the GPL that contain the word GNU, you type

```
egrep 'GNU' /usr/doc/copyright/GPL
```

`egrep` will print the lines to standard output. If you want all lines that contain `freedom` followed by some indeterminate text, followed by `GNU`, you can do this:

```
egrep 'freedom.*GNU' /usr/doc/copyright/GPL
```

The . means "any character," and the * means "zero or more of the preceding thing," in this case "zero or more of any character." So `.*` matches pretty much any text at all. `egrep` only matches on a line-by-line basis, so `freedom` and `GNU` have to be on the same line.

Here's a summary of regular expression metacharacters:

. Matches any single character except newline.

* Matches zero or more occurrences of the preceding thing. So the expression `a*` matches zero or more lowercase a, and `.*` matches zero or more characters.

[*characters*] The brackets must contain one or more characters; the whole bracketed expression matches exactly one character out of the set. So `[abc]` matches one a, one b, or one c; it does not match zero characters, and it does not match a character other than these three.

^ Anchors your search at the beginning of the line. The expression `^The` matches `The` when it appears at the beginning of a line; there can't be spaces or other text before `The`. If you want to allow spaces, you can permit 0 or more space characters like this: `^ *The`.

\$ Anchors at the end of the line. `end$` requires the text `end` to be at the end of the line, with no intervening spaces or text.

[^*characters*] This reverses the sense of a bracketed character list. So `[^abc]` matches any single character, *except* a, b, or c.

[*character-character*] You can include ranges in a bracketed character list. To match any lowercase letter, use `[a-z]`. You can have more than one range; so to match the first three or last three letters of the alphabet, try `[a-cx-z]`. To get any letter, any case, try `[a-zA-Z]`. You can mix ranges with single characters and with the

^metacharacter; for example, [^a-zBZ] means "anything except a lowercase letter, capital B, or capital Z."

() You can use parentheses to group parts of the regular expression, just as you do in a mathematical expression.

|| means "or." You can use it to provide a series of alternative expressions. Usually you want to put the alternatives in parentheses, like this: c(ad|ab|at) matches cad or cab or cat. Without the parentheses, it would match cad or ab or at instead

\Escapes any special characters; if you want to find a literal *, you type *. The slash means to ignore *'s usual special meaning.

Here are some more examples to help you get a feel for things:

c.pe matches cope, cape, caper.

c\ .pe matches c.pe, c.per.

sto*p matches stp, stop, stoop.

car.*n matches carton, cartoon, carmen.

xyz.* matches xyz and anything after it; some tools, like egrep, only match until the end of the line.

^The matches The at the beginning of a line.

atime$ matches atime at the end of a line.

^Only$ matches a line that consists solely of the word Only – no spaces, no other characters, nothing. Only Only is allowed.

b[aou]rn matches barn, born, burn.

Ver[D-F] matches VerD, VerE, VerF.

Ver[^0-9] matches Ver followed by any non-digit.

the[ir][re] matches their, therr, there, theie.

[A-Za-z][A-Za-z]* matches any word which consists of only letters, and at least one letter. It will not match numbers or spaces.

13.2   Advanced Files

Now that you have a basic understanding of files, it is time to learn more advanced things about them.

13.2.1   The Real Nature of Files: Hard Links and Inodes

Each file on your system is represented by an *inode* (for Information Node; pronounced "eye-node"). An inode contains all the information about the file. However, the inode is not directly visible. Instead, each inode is linked into the filesystem by one or more *hard links*. Hard links contain the name of the file and the inode number. The inode contains the file itself, i.e., the location of the information being stored on disk, its access permissions, the file type, and so on. The system can find any inode if it has the inode number.

A single file can have more than one hard link. What this means is that multiple filenames refer to the same file (that is, they are associated with the same inode number). However, you can't make hard links across filesystems: All hard references to a particular file (inode) must be on the same filesystem. This is because each filesystem has its own set of inodes, and there can be duplicate inode numbers on different filesystems.

Because all hard links to a given inode refer to *the same file*, you can make changes to the file, referring to it by one name, and then see those changes when referring to it by a different name. Try this:

```
cd; echo "hello" > firstlink
```

cd to your home directory and create a file called `firstlink` containing the word "hello." What you've actually done is redirect the output of echo (echo just echoes back what you give to it), placing the output in `firstlink`. See the chapter on shells for a full explanation.

```
cat firstlink
```

Confirms the contents of `firstlink`.

```
ln firstlink secondlink
```

Creates a hard link: `secondlink` now points to the same inode as `firstlink`.

```
cat secondlink
```

Confirms that `secondlink` is the same as `firstlink`.

```
ls -l
```

Notice that the number of hard links listed for `firstlink` and secondlinkfiles!inodes is 2.

```
echo "change" >> secondlink
```

This is another shell redirection trick (don't worry about the details). You've appended the word "change" to `secondlink`. Confirm this with `cat secondlink`.

```
cat firstlink
```

`firstlink` also has the word "change" appended! That's because `firstlink` and `secondlink` refer to *the same file*. It doesn't matter what you call it when you change it.

```
chmod a+rwx firstlink
```

Changes permissions on `firstlink`. Enter the command `ls -l` to confirm that permissions on `secondlink` were also changed. This means that permissions information is stored in the inode, not in links.

```
rm firstlink
```

Deletes this link. This is a subtlety of `rm`. It really removes links, not files. Now type `ls -l` and notice that `secondlink` is still there. Also notice that the number of hard links for `secondlink` has been reduced to one.

```
rm secondlink
```

Deletes the other link. When there are no more links to a file, Linux deletes the file itself, that is, its inode.

All files work like this – even special types of files such as devices (e.g. `/dev/hda`).

A directory is simply a list of filenames and inode numbers, that is, a list of hard links. When you create a hard link, you're just adding a name-number pair to a directory. When you delete a file, you're just removing a hard link from a directory.

13.2.2   Types of Files

One detail we've been concealing up to now is that the Linux kernel considers nearly everything to be a file. That includes directories and devices: They're just special kinds of files.

As you may remember, the first character of an `ls -l` display represents the type of the file. For an ordinary file, this will be simply `-`. Other possibilities include the following:

ddirectory

lsymbolic link

bblock device

ccharacter device

pnamed pipe

ssocket

Symbolic Links

Symbolic links (also called "symlinks" or "soft links") are the other kind of link besides hard links. A symlink is a special file that "points to" a hard link on any mounted filesystem. When you try to read the contents of a symlink, it gives the contents of the file it's pointing to rather than the contents of the symlink itself. Because directories, devices, and other symlinks are types of files, you can point a symlink at any of those things.

So a hard link is a filename and an inode number. A file is really an inode: a location on disk, file type, permissions mode, etc. A symlink is an inode that contains the name of a hard link. A symlink pairs one filename with a second filename, whereas a hard link pairs a filename with an inode number.

All hard links to the same file have equal status. That is, one is as good as another; if you perform any operation on one, it's just the same as performing that operation on any of the others. This is because the hard links all refer to the same inode. Operations on symlinks, on the other hand, sometimes affect the symlink's own inode (the one containing the name of a hard link) and sometimes affect the hard link being pointed to.

There are a number of important differences between symlinks and hard links.

Symlinks can cross filesystems. This is because they contain complete filenames, starting with the root directory, and all complete filenames are unique. Because hard links point to inode numbers, and inode numbers are unique only within a single filesystem, they would be ambiguous if the filesystem wasn't known.

You can make symlinks to directories, but you can't make hard links to them. Each directory has hard links – its listing in its parent directory, its . entry, and the .. entry in each of its subdirectories – but to impose order on the filesystem, no other hard links to directories are allowed. Consequently, the number of files in a directory is equal to the number of hard links to that directory minus two (you subtract the directory's name and the . link). comparing!hard links and symlinks You can only make a hard link to a file that exists, because there must be an inode number to refer to. However, you can make a symlink to any filename, whether or not there actually is such a filename.

Removing a symlink removes only the link. It has no effect on the linked-to file. Removing the only hard link to a file removes the file.

Try this:

```
cd; ln -s /tmp/me MyTmp
```

cd to your home directory. ln with the -s option makes a symbolic link – in this case, one called MyTmp that points to the filename /tmp/me.

```
ls -l MyTmp
```

Output should look like this:

```
lrwxrwxrwx 1 havoc havoc 7 Dec 6 12:50 MyTmp -> /tmp/me
```

The date and user/group names will be different for you, of course. Notice that the file type is l, indicating that this is a symbolic link. Also notice the permissions: Symbolic links always have these permissions. If you attempt to chmod a symlink, you'll actually change the permissions on the file being pointed to.

    chmod 700 MyTmp

You will get a No such file or directory error, because the file /tmp/me doesn't exist. Notice that you could create a symlink to it anyway.

    mkdir /tmp/me

Creates the directory /tmp/me.

    chmod 700 MyTmp

Should work now.

    touch MyTmp/myfile

Creates a file in MyTmp.

    ls /tmp/me

The file is actually created in /tmp/me.

    rm MyTmp

Removes the symbolic link. Notice that this removes the link, not what it points to. Thus you use rm not rmdir.

    rm /tmp/me/myfile; rmdir /tmp/me

Lets you clean up after yourself. symlinks!removing

Device Files

Device files refer to physical or virtual devices on your system, such as your hard disk, video card, screen, and keyboard. An example of a virtual device is the console, represented by /dev/console.

There are two kinds of devices:character and block. *Character devices* can be accessed one character at a time. Remember the smallest unit of data that can be written to or read from the device is a character (byte).

Block devices must be accessed in larger units called blocks, which contain a number of characters. Your hard disk is a block device.

You can read and write device files just as you can from other kinds of files, though the file may well contain some strange incomprehensible-to-humans gibberish. Writing random data to these files is probably a bad idea. Sometimes it's useful, though. For example, you can dump a postscript file into the printer device /dev/lp0 or send modem commands to the device file for the appropriate serial port.

/dev/null   /dev/null is a special device file that discards anything you write to it. If you don't want something, throw it in /dev/null. It's essentially a bottomless pit. If you read /dev/null, you'll get an end-of-file (EOF) character immediately. /dev/zero is similar, except that you read from it you get the \0 character (not the same as the number zero).

Named Pipes (FIFOs)

A named pipe is a file that acts like a pipe. You put something into the file, and it comes out the other end. Thus it's called a FIFO, or First-In-First-Out, because the first thing you put in the pipe is the first thing to come out the other end.

If you write to a named pipe, the process that is writing to the pipe doesn't terminate until the information being written is read from the pipe. If you read from a named pipe, the reading process waits until there's something to read before terminating. The size of the pipe is always zero: It doesn't store data, it just links two processes like the shell |. However, because this pipe has a name, the two processes don't have to be on the same command line or even be run by the same user.

You can try it by doing the following:

```
cd; mkfifo mypipe
```

Makes the pipe.

```
echo "hello" > mypipe &
```

Puts a process in the background that tries to write "hello" to the pipe. Notice that the process doesn't return from the background; it is waiting for someone to read from the pipe.

```
cat mypipe
```

At this point, the echo process should return, because cat read from the pipe, and the cat process will print hello.

```
rm mypipe
```

You can delete pipes just like any other file.

Sockets

Sockets are similar to pipes, only they work over the network. This is how your computer does networking. You may have heard of "WinSock," which is sockets for Windows.

We won't go into these further because you probably won't have occasion to use them unless you're programming. However, if you see a file marked with type son your computer, you know what it is.

13.2.3   The `proc` Filesystem

The Linux kernel makes a special filesystem available, which is mounted under /proc on Debian systems. This is a "pseudo-filesystem" because it doesn't really exist on any of your physical devices.

The `proc` filesystem contains information about the system and running processes. Some of the "files" in /proc are reasonably understandable to humans (try typing `cat /proc/meminfo` or `cat /proc/cpuinfo`); others are arcane collections of numbers. Often, system utilities use these to gather information and present it to you in a more understandable way.

People frequently panic when they notice one file in particular – /proc/kcore – which is generally huge. This is (more or less) a copy of the contents of your computer's memory. It's used to debug the kernel. It doesn't actually exist anywhere, so don't worry about its size.

If you want to know about all the things in /proc, type `man 5 proc`.

13.2.4   Large-Scale Copying

Sometimes you may want to copy one directory to another location. Maybe you're adding a new hard disk and you want to copy /usr/local to it. There are several ways you can do this.

The first is to use `cp`. The command `cp -a` will tell `cp` to do a copy preserving all the information it can. So, you might use

```
cp -a /usr/local /destination
```

However, there are some things that `cp -a` won't catch[1]. So, the best way to do a large copy job is to chain two `tar` commands together, like so:

```
tar -cSpf - /usr/local | tar -xvSpf -
-C /destination
```

The first `tar` command will archive the existing directory and pipe it to the second. The second command will unpack the archive into the location you specify with -C.

13.3   Security

Back in section 7.1 on page 71, we discussed file permissions in Linux. This is a fundamental way to keep your system secure. If you are running a multi-user system or a server, it is important to make sure that permissions are correct. A good rule of thumb is to set files to have the minimum permissions necessary for use.

---

1. Sparse files and hard links are two examples.

If you are running a network server, there are some other things to be aware of as well. First, you ought to uninstall or turn off any network services you're not using. A good place to start is the file /etc/inetd.conf; you can probably disable some of these. For most network services, it's also possible to control who has access to them; the /etc/hosts.allow and /etc/hosts.deny files (documented in man 5 hosts_access) can control who has access to which services. You also ought to keep up-to-date with patches or updates to Debian; these can be found on your nearest Debian FTP mirror.

Some other commonsense rules apply:

- Never tell anyone your password.

- Never send your password in cleartext across the Internet by using something like telnet or FTP. Instead, use encrypted protocols or avoid logging in remotely.

- Avoid using root as much as possible.

- Don't install untrusted software, and don't install it as root.

- Avoid making things world-writable whenever possible. /tmp is one exception to this rule.

While this is probably not of as much use to somebody not running a server, it is still pays to know a bit about security. Debian's security mechanism is what protects your system from many viruses.

13.4   Software Development with Debian

Debian makes a great platform for software development and programming. Among the languages and near-languages it supports are: C, C++, Objective-C, Perl, Python, m4, Ada, Pascal, Java, awk, Tcl/Tk, SQL, assembler, Bourne shell, csh, and more. Writing programs is beyond the scope of this book, but here are some of the more popular development programs in Debian:

gccThe GNU C Compiler, a modern optimizing C compiler.

g++The C++ compiler from the gcc line.

cppThe C preprocessor from gcc.

perlThe Perl interpreter. Perl is a great "glue" language.

gdbGNU Debugger, used to debug programs in many different languages.

gprofUsed for profiling, this program helps you to find ways to improve the performance of your programs.

emacsGNU Emacs is a programmers' editor and IDE.

asThe GNU Assembler.

II

Reference

Reading Documentation and Getting Help

A.1 Kinds of Documentation

On Debian systems, you can find documentation in at least the following places:

- `man` pages, read with the `man` command.
- `info` pages, read with the `info` command.
- The `/usr/doc/`*package* directories, where *package* is the name of the Debian package.

  Tip:

  `zless` is useful for reading the files in `/usr/doc`; see section 8.1 on page 81 for details.

- `/usr/doc/HOWTO/`contains the Linux Documentation Project's HOWTO documents, if you've installed the Debian packages containing them.
- Many commands have an `-h` or `--help` option. Type the command name followed by one of these options to try it.

- The Debian Documentation Project[1] has written some manuals.
- The Debian support page[2] has a FAQ and other resources. You can also try the Linux web site[3].

The confusing variety of documentation sources exists for many reasons. For example, info is supposed to replace man, but man hasn't disappeared yet. However, it's nice to know that so much documentation exists!

So where to look for help? Here are some suggestions:

- Use the man pages and the --help or -h option to get a quick summary of a command's syntax and options. Also use man if a program doesn't yet have an info page.
- Use info if a program has info documentation.
- If neither of those works, look in /usr/doc/*packagename*.
- /usr/doc/*packagename* often has Debian-specific information, even if there's a man page or info page.
- Use the HOWTOs for instructions on how to set up a particular thing or for information on your particular hardware. For example, the Ethernet HOWTO has a wealth of information on Ethernet cards, and the PPP HOWTO explains in detail how to set up PPP.
- Use the Debian Documentation Project manuals for conceptual explanations and Debian-specific information.
- If all else fails, ask someone. See section A.1.3 on page 122.

Using man pages is discussed above in section 5.1 on page 49. It's very simple: press the space bar to go to the next page, and press q to quit reading. Using info, viewing files in /usr/doc, and asking for help from a person are all discussed in the remainder of this chapter.

A.1.1   Using info

info is the GNU documentation viewer. Some programs provide documentationin info format, and you can use info to view that documentation. You can start up the viewer by simply typing info, or by supplying a topic as well:

```
info emacs
```

You can also bring up the information on info itself, which includes a tutorial, like so:

1. http://www.debian.org/~elphick/ddp/
2. http://www.debian.org/support/
3. http://www.linux.org/

```
info info
```

Now, you may navigate with these keys:

arrowsMove the cursor around the document
m RET Select the menu item that's at the cursor
uMove "up" in the document
nMove to the next page
pMove to the previous page
sSearch for something
gGo to a specific page
qQuit info

You might notice that the top line of the screen indicates the next, previous, and "up" pages, corresponding nicely to the actions for the n, p, and u keys.

A.1.2   HOWTOs

In addition to their books, the Linux Documentation Project has made a series of short documents describing how to set up particular aspects of GNU/Linux. For instance, the SCSI-HOWTO describes some of the complications of using SCSI – a standard way of talking to devices – with GNU/Linux. In general, the HOWTOs have more specific information about particular hardware configurations and will be more up to date than this manual.

There are Debian packages for the HOWTOs. `doc-linux-text` contains the various HOWTOs in text form; the `doc-linux-html` package contains the HOWTOs in (surprise!) browsable HTML format. Note also that Debian has packaged translations of the HOWTOs in various languages that you may prefer if English is not your native language. Debian has packages for the German, French, Spanish, Italian, Japanese, Korean, Polish, Swedish and Chinese versions of the HOWTOs. These are usually available in the package `doc-linux-languagecode`, where `languagecode` is `fr` for French, `es` for Spanish, etc. If you've installed one of these, you should have them in `/usr/doc/HOWTO`. However, you may be able to find more recent versions on the Net at the LDP homepage[4].

---

4. http://metalab.unc.edu/LDP/

A.1.3   Personal Help

The correct place to ask for help with Debian is the `debian-user` mailing list at `debian-user@lists.debian.org`. If you know how to use IRC (Internet Relay Chat), you can use the `#debian` channel on `irc.debian.org`. You can find general GNU/Linux help on the `comp.os.linux.*` USENET hierarchy. It is also possible to hire paid consultants to provide guaranteed support services. The Debian website[5] has more information on many of these resources.

Again, please *do not* ask the authors of this book for help. We probably don't know the answer to your specific problem anyway; if you mail `debian-user`, you will get higher-quality responses, and more quickly.

Always be polite and make an effort to help yourself by reading the documentation. Remember, Debian is a volunteer effort and people are doing you a favor by giving their time to help you. Many of them charge hundreds of dollars for the same services during the day.

Tips for asking questions

- Read the obvious documentation first. Things like command options and what a command does will be covered there. This includes manpages and info documentation.

- Check the HOWTO documents if your question is about setting up something such as PPP or Ethernet.

- Try to be sure the answer isn't in this book.

- Don't be afraid to ask, after you've made a basic effort to look it up.

- Don't be afraid to ask for conceptual explanations, advice, and other things not often found in the documentation.

- Include any information that seems relevant. You'll almost always want to mention the version of Debian you're using. You may also want to mention the version of any pertinent packages: The command `dpkg -l *packagename*` will tell you this. It's also useful to say what you've tried so far and what happened. Please include the exact error messages, if any.

- Don't apologize for being new to Linux. There's no reason everyone should be a GNU/Linux expert to use it, any more than everyone should be a mechanic to use a car.

---

5. http://www.debian.org/

- Don't post or mail in HTML. Some versions of Netscape and Internet Explorer will post in HTML rather than plain text. Most people will not even read these posts because the posts are difficult to read in most mail programs. There should be a setting somewhere in the preferences to disable HTML.

- Be polite. Remember that Debian is an all-volunteer effort, and anyone who helps you is doing so on his or her time out of kindness.

- Re-mail your question to the list if you've gotten no responses after several days. Perhaps there were lots of messages and it was overlooked. Or perhaps no one knows the answer – if no one answers the second time, this is a good bet. You might want to try including more information the second time.

- Answer questions yourself when you know the answer. Debian depends on everyone doing his or her part. If you ask a question, and later on someone else asks the same question, you'll know how to answer it. Do so!

A.1.4   Getting Information from the System

When diagnosing problems or asking for help, you'll need to get information about your system. Here are some ways to do so:

- Examine the files in `/var/log/`.
- Examine the output of the `dmesg` command.
- Run `uname -a`.

B

Troubleshooting

In Debian, as in life, things don't always work as you might expect or want them to. While Debian has a well-deserved reputation for being rock-solid and stable, sometimes its reaction to your commands may be unexpected. Here, we try to shed some light on the most common problems that people encounter.

B.1 Common Difficulties

This section provides some tips for handling some of the most frequently experienced difficulties users have encountered.

B.1.1 Working with Strangely-Named Files

Occasionally, you may find that you have accidentally created a file that contains a character not normally found in a filename. Examples of this could include a space, a leading hyphen, or maybe a quotation mark. You may find that accessing, removing, or renaming these files can be difficult.

Here are some tips to help you:

- Try enclosing the filename in single quotation marks, like this:
  `less 'File With Spaces.txt'`
- Insert a ./ before the filename:
  `less './-a strange file.txt'`
- Use wildcards:
  `less File?With?Spaces.txt`
- Use a backslash before each unusual character:
  `less File\ With\ Spaces.txt`

B.1.2   Printing

One common source of trouble is the printing system in Debian. Traditionally, printing has been a powerful but complex aspect of Unix. However, Debian makes it easier. An easy way to print is with the package called `magicfilter`. `magicfilter` will ask you a few questions about your printer and then configure it for you. If you are having troubles printing, give `magicfilter` a try.

B.1.3   X Problems

Many questions revolve around X. Here are some general tips for things to try if you are having difficulties setting up the X Window system:

- For mouse problems, run `XF86Setup` and try the PS/2, Microsoft, MouseSystems, and Logitech options. Most mice will fit under one of these. Also, the device for your mouse is `/dev/psaux` for PS/2 mice and a serial port such as `/dev/ttyS0` for serial mice.
- If you don't know what video chipset you have, try running `SuperProbe`; it can often figure this out for you.
- If your screen doesn't have a lot of color, try selecting a different video card or tell X how much video RAM you have.
- If your screen goes blank or has unreadable text when you start X, you probably selected an incorrect refresh rate. Go back to `XF86Setup` or `xf86config` and double-check those settings.
- `xvidtune` can help if the image on the screen is shifted too far to the left or right, is too high or low, or is too narrow or wide.
- `xdpyinfo` can give information about a running X session.
- `XF86Setup` can set your default color depth.
- You can select your default window manager by editing `/etc/X11/window-managers`.

- `/var/log/xdm-errors` can contain useful information if you are having trouble getting `xdm` to start properly.

As a final reminder, try the `XF86Setup` or `xf86config` tools for configuring or reconfiguring X for your hardware.

B.2   Troubleshooting the Boot Process

If you have problems during the boot process, such as the kernel hangs during the boot process, the kernel doesn't recognize peripherals you actually have, or drives are not recognized properly, the first things to check are the boot parameters. They can be found by pressing **F1** when booting from the rescue disk.

Often, problems can be solved by removing add-ons and peripherals and then booting again. Internal modems, sound cards, and Plug-n-Play devices are especially problematic.

Tecras and other notebooks, and some non-portables fail to flush the cache when switching on the A20 gate, which is provoked by bzImage kernels but not by zImage kernels. If your computer suffers from this problem, you'll see a message during boot saying `A20 gating failed`. In this case, you'll have to use the 'tecra' boot images.

If you still have problems, please submit a bug report. Send an email to `submit@bugs.debian.org`. You *must* include the following as the first lines of the email:

```
Package: boot-floppies
Version: version
```

Make sure you fill in *version* with the version of the boot-floppies set that you used. If you don't know the version, use the date you downloaded the floppies, and include the distribution you got them from (e.g., "stable" or "frozen").

You should also include the following information in your bug report:

architecturei386

modelyour general hardware vendor and model

memoryamount of RAM

scsiSCSI host adapter, if any

cd-romCD-ROM model and interface type, i.e., ATAPI

network cardnetwork interface card, if any

pcmciadetails of any PCMCIA devices

Depending on the nature of the bug, it also might be useful to report the disk model, the disk capacity, and the model of video card.

In the bug report, describe what the problem is, including the last visible kernel messages in the event of a kernel hang. Describe the steps you performed that put the system into the problem state.

C

Booting the System

This appendix describes what happens during the GNU/Linux boot process.

How you boot your system depends on how you set things up when you installed Debian. Most likely, you just turn the computer on. But you may have to insert a floppy disk first.

Linux is loaded by a program called LILO, or LInux LOader. LILO can also load other operating systems and ask you which system you'd like to load.

The first thing that happens when you turn on an Intel PC is that the BIOS executes. BIOS stands for Basic Input Output System. It's a program permanently stored in the computer on read-only chips. It performs some minimal tests and then looks for a floppy disk in the first disk drive. If it finds one, it looks for a "boot sector" on that disk and starts executing code from it, if there is any. If there is a disk but no boot sector, the BIOS will print a message like this: `Non-system disk or disk error`. Removing the disk and pressing a key will cause the boot process to resume.

If there isn't a floppy disk in the drive, the BIOS looks for a master boot record (MBR) on the hard disk. It will start executing the code found there, which loads the operating system. On GNU/Linux systems, LILO can occupy the MBR and will load GNU/Linux.

Thus, if you opted to install LILO on your hard drive, you should see the word LILO as your computer starts up. At that point, you can press the left Shift key to select which operating system to load or press Tab to see a list of options. Type in one of those options and press Enter. LILO will boot the requested operating system.

If you don't press the Shift key, LILO will automatically load the default operating system after about 5 seconds. If you like, you can change what system LILO loads automatically, which systems it knows how to load, and how long it waits before loading one automatically.

If you didn't install LILO on your hard drive, you probably created a *boot disk*. The boot disk will have LILO on it. All you have to do is insert the disk before you turn on your computer, and the BIOS will find it before it checks the MBR on the hard drive. To return to a non-Linux OS, take out the boot disk and restart the computer. From Linux, be sure you follow the proper procedure for restarting; see section 4.5 on page 47 for details.

LILO loads the Linux kernel from disk and then lets the kernel take over. (The kernel is the central program of the operating system, which is in control of all other programs.) The kernel discards the BIOS and LILO.

On non-Intel platforms, things work a little differently. But once you boot, everything is more or less the same.

Linux looks at the type of hardware it's running on. It wants to know what type of hard disks you have, whether or not you have a bus mouse, whether or not you're on a network, and other bits of trivia like that. Linux can't remember things between boots, so it has to ask these questions each time it starts up. Luckily, it isn't asking *you* these questions – it's asking the hardware! While it boots, the Linux kernel will print messages on the screen describing what it's doing.

The query process can cause problems with your system, but if it was going to, it probably would have when you first installed GNU/Linux. If you're having problems, consult the installation instructions or ask questions on a mailing list.

The kernel merely manages other programs, so once it is satisfied everything is okay, it must start another program to do anything useful. The program the kernel starts is called init. After the kernel starts init, it never starts another program. The kernel becomes a manager and a provider of services.

Once init is started, it runs a number of scripts (files containing commands), which prepare the system to be used. They do some routine maintenance and start up a lot of programs that do things like display a login prompt, listen for network connections, and keep a log of the computer's activities.

The GNU General Public License

GNU GENERAL PUBLIC LICENSE
Version 2, June 1991

Copyright (C) 1989, 1991 Free Software Foundation, Inc.
59 Temple Place, Suite 330, Boston,
MA 02111-1307   USA
Everyone is permitted to copy and distribute verbatim copies
of this license document, but changing it is not allowed.

Preamble

The licenses for most software are designed to take away your
freedom to share and change it. By contrast, the GNU General Public
License is intended to guarantee your freedom to share and change free
software--to make sure the software is free for all its users. This
General Public License applies to most of the Free Software
Foundation's software and to any other program whose authors commit to
using it. (Some other Free Software Foundation software is covered by
the GNU Library General Public License instead.) You can apply it to
your programs, too.

When we speak of free software, we are referring to freedom, not price. Our General Public Licenses are designed to make sure that you have the freedom to distribute copies of free software (and charge for this service if you wish), that you receive source code or can get it if you want it, that you can change the software or use pieces of it in new free programs; and that you know you can do these things.

To protect your rights, we need to make restrictions that forbid anyone to deny you these rights or to ask you to surrender the rights. These restrictions translate to certain responsibilities for you if you distribute copies of the software, or if you modify it.

For example, if you distribute copies of such a program, whether gratis or for a fee, you must give the recipients all the rights that you have. You must make sure that they, too, receive or can get the source code. And you must show them these terms so they know their rights.

We protect your rights with two steps: (1) copyright the software, and (2) offer you this license which gives you legal permission to copy, distribute and/or modify the software.

Also, for each author's protection and ours, we want to make certain that everyone understands that there is no warranty for this free software. If the software is modified by someone else and passed on, we want its recipients to know that what they have is not the original, so that any problems introduced by others will not reflect on the original authors' reputations.

Finally, any free program is threatened constantly by software patents. We wish to avoid the danger that redistributors of a free program will individually obtain patent licenses, in effect making the program proprietary. To prevent this, we have made it clear that any patent must be licensed for everyone's free use or not licensed at all.

The precise terms and conditions for copying, distribution and modification follow.

GNU GENERAL PUBLIC LICENSE
TERMS AND CONDITIONS FOR COPYING, DISTRIBUTION AND MODIFICATION

0. This License applies to any program or other work which contains a notice placed by the copyright holder saying it may be distributed under the terms of this General Public License. The "Program", below, refers to any such program or work, and a "work based on the Program"

means either the Program or any derivative work under copyright law:
that is to say, a work containing the Program or a portion of it,
either verbatim or with modifications and/or translated into another
language. (Hereinafter, translation is included without limitation in
the term "modification".) Each licensee is addressed as "you".

Activities other than copying, distribution and modification are not
covered by this License; they are outside its scope. The act of
running the Program is not restricted, and the output from the Program
is covered only if its contents constitute a work based on the
Program (independent of having been made by running the Program).
Whether that is true depends on what the Program does.

   1. You may copy and distribute verbatim copies of the Program's
source code as you receive it, in any medium, provided that you
conspicuously and appropriately publish on each copy an appropriate
copyright notice and disclaimer of warranty; keep intact all the
notices that refer to this License and to the absence of any warranty;
and give any other recipients of the Program a copy of this License
along with the Program.

You may charge a fee for the physical act of transferring a copy, and
you may at your option offer warranty protection in exchange for a fee.

   2. You may modify your copy or copies of the Program or any portion
of it, thus forming a work based on the Program, and copy and
distribute such modifications or work under the terms of Section 1
above, provided that you also meet all of these conditions:

   a) You must cause the modified files to carry prominent notices
   stating that you changed the files and the date of any change.

   b) You must cause any work that you distribute or publish, that in
   whole or in part contains or is derived from the Program or any
   part thereof, to be licensed as a whole at no charge to all third
   parties under the terms of this License.

   c) If the modified program normally reads commands interactively
   when run, you must cause it, when started running for such
   interactive use in the most ordinary way, to print or display an
   announcement including an appropriate copyright notice and a
   notice that there is no warranty (or else, saying that you provide
   a warranty) and that users may redistribute the program under
   these conditions, and telling the user how to view a copy of this
   License. (Exception: if the Program itself is interactive but
   does not normally print such an announcement, your work based on

the Program is not required to print an announcement.)

These requirements apply to the modified work as a whole. If identifiable sections of that work are not derived from the Program, and can be reasonably considered independent and separate works in themselves, then this License, and its terms, do not apply to those sections when you distribute them as separate works. But when you distribute the same sections as part of a whole which is a work based on the Program, the distribution of the whole must be on the terms of this License, whose permissions for other licensees extend to the entire whole, and thus to each and every part regardless of who wrote it.

Thus, it is not the intent of this section to claim rights or contest your rights to work written entirely by you; rather, the intent is to exercise the right to control the distribution of derivative or collective works based on the Program.

In addition, mere aggregation of another work not based on the Program with the Program (or with a work based on the Program) on a volume of a storage or distribution medium does not bring the other work under the scope of this License.

3. You may copy and distribute the Program (or a work based on it, under Section 2) in object code or executable form under the terms of Sections 1 and 2 above provided that you also do one of the following:

a) Accompany it with the complete corresponding machine-readable source code, which must be distributed under the terms of Sections 1 and 2 above on a medium customarily used for software interchange; or,

b) Accompany it with a written offer, valid for at least three years, to give any third party, for a charge no more than your cost of physically performing source distribution, a complete machine-readable copy of the corresponding source code, to be distributed under the terms of Sections 1 and 2 above on a medium customarily used for software interchange; or,

c) Accompany it with the information you received as to the offer to distribute corresponding source code. (This alternative is allowed only for noncommercial distribution and only if you received the program in object code or executable form with such an offer, in accord with Subsection b above.)

The source code for a work means the preferred form of the work for making modifications to it. For an executable work, complete source

code means all the source code for all modules it contains, plus any
associated interface definition files, plus the scripts used to
control compilation and installation of the executable. However, as a
special exception, the source code distributed need not include
anything that is normally distributed (in either source or binary
form) with the major components (compiler, kernel, and so on) of the
operating system on which the executable runs, unless that component
itself accompanies the executable.

If distribution of executable or object code is made by offering
access to copy from a designated place, then offering equivalent
access to copy the source code from the same place counts as
distribution of the source code, even though third parties are not
compelled to copy the source along with the object code.

   4. You may not copy, modify, sublicense, or distribute the Program
except as expressly provided under this License. Any attempt
otherwise to copy, modify, sublicense or distribute the Program is
void, and will automatically terminate your rights under this License.
However, parties who have received copies, or rights, from you under
this License will not have their licenses terminated so long as such
parties remain in full compliance.

   5. You are not required to accept this License, since you have not
signed it. However, nothing else grants you permission to modify or
distribute the Program or its derivative works. These actions are
prohibited by law if you do not accept this License. Therefore, by
modifying or distributing the Program (or any work based on the
Program), you indicate your acceptance of this License to do so, and
all its terms and conditions for copying, distributing or modifying
the Program or works based on it.

   6. Each time you redistribute the Program (or any work based on the
Program), the recipient automatically receives a license from the
original licensor to copy, distribute or modify the Program subject to
these terms and conditions. You may not impose any further
restrictions on the recipients' exercise of the rights granted herein.
You are not responsible for enforcing compliance by third parties to
this License.

   7. If, as a consequence of a court judgment or allegation of patent
infringement or for any other reason (not limited to patent issues),
conditions are imposed on you (whether by court order, agreement or
otherwise) that contradict the conditions of this License, they do not
excuse you from the conditions of this License. If you cannot
distribute so as to satisfy simultaneously your obligations under this

License and any other pertinent obligations, then as a consequence you
may not distribute the Program at all. For example, if a patent
license would not permit royalty-free redistribution of the Program by
all those who receive copies directly or indirectly through you, then
the only way you could satisfy both it and this License would be to
refrain entirely from distribution of the Program.

If any portion of this section is held invalid or unenforceable under
any particular circumstance, the balance of the section is intended to
apply and the section as a whole is intended to apply in other
circumstances.

It is not the purpose of this section to induce you to infringe any
patents or other property right claims or to contest validity of any
such claims; this section has the sole purpose of protecting the
integrity of the free software distribution system, which is
implemented by public license practices. Many people have made
generous contributions to the wide range of software distributed
through that system in reliance on consistent application of that
system; it is up to the author/donor to decide if he or she is willing
to distribute software through any other system and a licensee cannot
impose that choice.

This section is intended to make thoroughly clear what is believed to
be a consequence of the rest of this License.

   8. If the distribution and/or use of the Program is restricted in
certain countries either by patents or by copyrighted interfaces, the
original copyright holder who places the Program under this License
may add an explicit geographical distribution limitation excluding
those countries, so that distribution is permitted only in or among
countries not thus excluded. In such case, this License incorporates
the limitation as if written in the body of this License.

   9. The Free Software Foundation may publish revised and/or new versions
of the General Public License from time to time. Such new versions will
be similar in spirit to the present version, but may differ in detail to
address new problems or concerns.

Each version is given a distinguishing version number. If the Program
specifies a version number of this License which applies to it and "any
later version", you have the option of following the terms and conditions
either of that version or of any later version published by the Free
Software Foundation. If the Program does not specify a version number of
this License, you may choose any version ever published by the Free
Software Foundation.

10. If you wish to incorporate parts of the Program into other free
programs whose distribution conditions are different, write to the author
to ask for permission. For software which is copyrighted by the Free
Software Foundation, write to the Free Software Foundation; we sometimes
make exceptions for this. Our decision will be guided by the two goals
of preserving the free status of all derivatives of our free software and
of promoting the sharing and reuse of software generally.

NO WARRANTY

11. BECAUSE THE PROGRAM IS LICENSED FREE OF CHARGE, THERE IS NO WARRANTY
FOR THE PROGRAM, TO THE EXTENT PERMITTED BY APPLICABLE LAW. EXCEPT WHEN
OTHERWISE STATED IN WRITING THE COPYRIGHT HOLDERS AND/OR OTHER PARTIES
PROVIDE THE PROGRAM "AS IS" WITHOUT WARRANTY OF ANY KIND, EITHER EXPRESSED
OR IMPLIED, INCLUDING, BUT NOT LIMITED TO, THE IMPLIED WARRANTIES OF
MERCHANTABILITY AND FITNESS FOR A PARTICULAR PURPOSE. THE ENTIRE RISK AS
TO THE QUALITY AND PERFORMANCE OF THE PROGRAM IS WITH YOU. SHOULD THE
PROGRAM PROVE DEFECTIVE, YOU ASSUME THE COST OF ALL NECESSARY SERVICING,
REPAIR OR CORRECTION.

12. IN NO EVENT UNLESS REQUIRED BY APPLICABLE LAW OR AGREED TO IN
WRITING WILL ANY COPYRIGHT HOLDER, OR ANY OTHER PARTY WHO MAY MODIFY AND/
OR REDISTRIBUTE THE PROGRAM AS PERMITTED ABOVE, BE LIABLE TO YOU FOR
DAMAGES, INCLUDING ANY GENERAL, SPECIAL, INCIDENTAL OR CONSEQUENTIAL
DAMAGES ARISING OUT OF THE USE OR INABILITY TO USE THE PROGRAM (INCLUDING
BUT NOT LIMITED TO LOSS OF DATA OR DATA BEING RENDERED INACCURATE OR
LOSSES SUSTAINED BY YOU OR THIRD PARTIES OR A FAILURE OF THE PROGRAM TO
OPERATE WITH ANY OTHER PROGRAMS), EVEN IF SUCH HOLDER OR OTHER PARTY
HAS BEEN ADVISED OF THE POSSIBILITY OF SUCH DAMAGES.

END OF TERMS AND CONDITIONS

How to Apply These Terms to Your New Programs

If you develop a new program, and you want it to be of the greatest
possible use to the public, the best way to achieve this is to make it
free software which everyone can redistribute and change under these
terms.

To do so, attach the following notices to the program. It is safest
to attach them to the start of each source file to most effectively
convey the exclusion of warranty; and each file should have at least
the "copyright" line and a pointer to where the full notice is found.

    <one line to give the program's name and a brief idea of what

it does.>
    Copyright (C) 19yy <name of author>

    This program is free software; you can redistribute it and/or modify
    it under the terms of the GNU General Public License as published by
    the Free Software Foundation; either version 2 of the License, or
    (at your option) any later version.

    This program is distributed in the hope that it will be useful,
    but WITHOUT ANY WARRANTY; without even the implied warranty of
    MERCHANTABILITY or FITNESS FOR A PARTICULAR PURPOSE. See the
    GNU General Public License for more details.

    You should have received a copy of the GNU General Public License
    along with this program; if not, write to the Free Software
    Foundation, Inc., 59 Temple Place, Suite 330, Boston, MA 02111-1307
USA

Also add information on how to contact you by electronic and paper mail.

If the program is interactive, make it output a short notice like this
when it starts in an interactive mode:

    Gnomovision version 69, Copyright (C) 19yy name of author
    Gnomovision comes with ABSOLUTELY NO WARRANTY; for details type
'show w'.
    This is free software, and you are welcome to redistribute it
    under certain conditions; type 'show c' for details.

The hypothetical commands 'show w' and 'show c' should show the
appropriate
parts of the General Public License. Of course, the commands you use may
be called something other than 'show w' and 'show c'; they could even be
mouse-clicks or menu items--whatever suits your program.

You should also get your employer (if you work as a programmer) or your
school, if any, to sign a "copyright disclaimer" for the program, if
necessary. Here is a sample; alter the names:

  Yoyodyne, Inc., hereby disclaims all copyright interest in the program
  'Gnomovision' (which makes passes at compilers) written by James Hacker.

  <signature of Ty Coon>, 1 April 1989
  Ty Coon, President of Vice

This General Public License does not permit incorporating your program into proprietary programs. If your program is a subroutine library, you may consider it more useful to permit linking proprietary applications with the library. If this is what you want to do, use the GNU Library General Public License instead of this License.

Symbols

A

M

T

U

V

New Riders

Books for Networking Professionals

Windows NT Titles

Windows NT TCP/IP

By Karanjit Siyan
1st Edition
480 pages, $29.99
ISBN: 1-56205-887-8

If you're still looking for good documentation on Microsoft TCP/IP, then look no further—this is your book. *Windows NT TCP/IP* cuts through the complexities and provides the most informative and complete reference book on Windows-based TCP/IP. Concepts essential to TCP/IP administration are explained thoroughly, then related to the practical use of Microsoft TCP/IP in a real-world networking environment. The book begins by covering TCP/IP architecture, advanced installation, and configuration issues, then moves on to routing with TCP/IP, DHCP Management, and WINS/DNS Name Resolution.

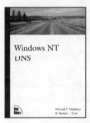

Windows NT DNS

By Michael Masterson, Herman L. Knief, Scott Vinick, and Eric Roul
1st Edition
340 pages, $29.99
ISBN: 1-56205-943-2

Have you ever opened a Windows NT book looking for detailed information about DNS only to discover that it doesn't even begin to scratch the surface? DNS is probably one of the most complicated subjects for NT administrators, and there are few books on the market that really address it in detail. This book answers your most complex DNS questions, focusing on the implementation of the Domain Name Service within Windows NT, treating it thoroughly from the viewpoint of an experienced Windows NT professional. Many detailed, real-world examples illustrate further the understanding of the material throughout. The book covers the details of how DNS functions within NT, then explores specific interactions with critical network components. Finally, proven procedures to design and set up DNS are demonstrated. You'll also find coverage of related topics, such as maintenance, security, and troubleshooting.

Windows NT Registry

By Sandra Osborne
1st Edition
564 pages, $29.99
ISBN: 1-56205-941-6

The NT Registry can be a very powerful tool for those capable of using it wisely. Unfortunately, there is very little information regarding the NT Registry, due to Microsoft's insistence that their source code be kept secret. If you're looking to optimize your use of the Registry, you're usually forced to search the Web for bits of information. This book is your resource. It covers critical issues and settings used for configuring network protocols, including NWLink, PTP, TCP/IP, and DHCP. This book approaches the material from a unique point of view, discussing the problems related to a particular component, and then discussing settings, which are the actual changes necessary for implementing robust solutions. There is also a comprehensive reference of Registry settings and commands, making this the perfect addition to your technical bookshelf.

Windows NT Performance

By Mark Edmead and Paul Hinsberg

1st Edition

288 pages, $29.99

ISBN: 1-56205-942-4

Performance monitoring is a little like preventative medicine for the administrator: No one enjoys a checkup, but it's a good thing to do on a regular basis. This book helps you focus on the critical aspects of improving the performance of your NT system, showing you how to monitor the system, implement benchmarking, and tune your network. The book is organized by resource components, which makes it easy to use as a reference tool.

Windows NT Terminal Server

By Ted Harwood

1st Edition

416 pages, $29.99

ISBN: 1-56205-944-0

It's no surprise that most administration headaches revolve around integration with other networks and clients. This book addresses these types of real-world issues on a case-by-case basis, giving tools and advice for solving each problem. The author also offers the real nuts and bolts of thin client administration on multiple systems, covering such relevant issues as installation, configuration, network connection, management, and application distribution.

Windows NT Security

By Richard Puckett

1st Edition Fall 1999

600 pages, $29.99

ISBN: 1-56205-945-9

Swiss cheese. That's what some people say Windows NT security is like. And they may be right, because they only know what the NT documentation says about implementing security. Who has the time to research alternatives; play around with the features, service packs, hot fixes, and add-on tools; and figure out what makes NT rock solid? Well, Richard Puckett does. He's been researching Windows NT security for the University of Virginia for a while now, and he's got pretty good news. He's going to show you how to make NT secure in your environment, and we mean really secure.

Windows NT Network Management

By Anil Desai

1st Edition Spring 1999

400 pages, $34.99

ISBN: 1-56205-946-7

Administering a Windows NT network is kind of like trying to herd cats—an impossible task characterized by constant motion, exhausting labor, and lots of hairballs. Author Anil Desai knows all about it—he's a Consulting Engineer for Sprint Paranet, and specializes in Windows NT implementation, integration, and management. So we asked him to put together a concise manual of best practices, a book of tools and ideas that other administrators can turn to again and again in managing their own NT networks. His experience shines through as he shares his secrets for reducing your organization's Total Cost of Ownership.

Planning for Windows 2000

By Jon Boggs, Eric K. Cone, Sergio Perez
1st Edition Spring 1999
400 pages, $29.99
ISBN: 0-7357-0048-6

Windows 2000 is poised to be one of the largest and most important software releases of the next decade, and you are charged with planning, testing, and deploying it in your enterprise. Are you ready? With this book, you will be. *Planning for Windows 2000* lets you know what the upgrade hurdles will be, informs you how to clear them, guides you through effective Active Directory design, and presents you with detailed rollout procedures.

MCSE Core NT Exams Essential Reference

By Matthew Shepker
1st Edition
256 pages, $19.99
ISBN: 0-7357-0006-0

You're sitting in the first session of your Networking Essentials class and the instructor starts talking about RAS and you have no idea what that means. You think about raising your hand to ask about RAS, but you reconsider—you'd feel pretty foolish asking a question in front of all these people. You turn to your handy *MCSE Core NT Exams Essential Reference* and find a quick summary on Remote Access Services. Question answered. It's a couple months later and you're taking your Networking Essentials exam the next day. You're reviewing practice tests and you keep forgetting the maximum lengths for the various commonly used cable types. Once again, you turn to the *MCSE Core NT Exams Essential Reference* and find a table on cables, including all of the characteristics you need to memorize in order to pass the test.

BackOffice Titles

Implementing Exchange Server

By Doug Hauger, Marywynne Leon, and William C. Wade III
1st Edition
400 pages, $29.99
ISBN: 1-56205-931-9

If you're interested in connectivity and maintenance issues for Exchange Server, then this book is for you. Exchange's power lies in its ability to be connected to multiple email subsystems to create a "universal email backbone." It's not unusual to have several different and complex systems all connected via email gateways, including Lotus Notes or cc:Mail, Microsoft Mail, legacy mainframe systems, and Internet mail. This book covers all of the problems and issues associated with getting an integrated system running smoothly and addresses troubleshooting and diagnosis of email problems with an eye towards prevention and best practices.

Exchange Server Administration

By Janice K. Howd
1st Edition Spring 1999
350 pages, $34.99
ISBN: 0-7357-0081-8

OK, you've got your Exchange Server installed and connected, now what? Email administration is one of the most critical networking jobs, and Exchange can be particularly troublesome in large, heterogenous environments. So Janice Howd, a noted consultant and teacher with over a decade of email administration experience, has put together this advanced, concise handbook for daily, periodic, and emergency administration. With in-depth coverage of topics like managing disk resources, replication, and disaster recovery, this is the one reference book every Exchange administrator needs.

SQL Server System Administration

By Sean Baird, Chris Miller, et al.

1st Edition

352 pages, $29.99

ISBN: 1-56205-955-6

How often does your SQL Server go down during the day when everyone wants to access the data? Do you spend most of your time being a "report monkey" for your co-workers and bosses? *SQL Server System Administration* helps you keep data consistently available to your users. This book omits the introductory information. The authors don't spend time explaining queries and how they work. Instead they focus on the information that you can't get anywhere else, like how to choose the correct replication topology and achieve high availability of information.

Internet Information Server Administration

By Kelli Adam, et. al.

1st Edition Fall 1999

300 pages, $29.99

ISBN: 0-7357-0022-2

Are the new Internet technologies in Internet Information Server giving you headaches? Does protecting security on the Web take up all of your time? Then this is the book for you. With hands-on configuration training, advanced study of the new protocols in IIS, and detailed instructions on authenticating users with the new Certificate Server and implementing and managing the new e-commerce features, *Internet Information Server Administration* gives you the real-life solutions you need. This definitive resource also prepares you for the release of Windows 2000 by giving you detailed advice on working with Microsoft Management Console, which was first used by IIS.

SMS Administration

By Wayne Koop and Brian Steck

1st Edition Fall 1999

350 pages, $29.99

ISBN: 0-7357-0082-6

Microsoft's new version of its Systems Management Server (SMS) is starting to turn heads. While complex, it's allowing administrators to lower their total cost of ownership and more efficiently manage clients, applications and support operations. So if your organization is using or implementing SMS, you'll need some expert advice. Wayne Koop and Brian Steck can help you get the most bang for your buck, with insight, expert tips, and real-world examples. Brian and Wayne are consultants specializing in SMS, having worked with Microsoft on one of the most complex SMS rollouts in the world, involving 32 countries, 15 languages, and thousands of clients.

Unix/Linux Titles

Solaris Essential Reference
By John P. Mulligan
1st Edition
350 pages, $24.95
ISBN: 0-7357-0023-0

Looking for the fastest, easiest way to find the Solaris command you need? Need a few pointers on shell scripting? How about advanced administration tips and sound, practical expertise on security issues? Are you looking for trustworthy information about available third-party software packages that will enhance your operating system? Author John Mulligan—creator of the popular Unofficial Guide to Solaris Web site (sun.icsnet.com)—delivers all that and more in one attractive, easy-to-use reference book. With clear and concise instructions on how to perform important administration and management tasks and key information on powerful commands and advanced topics, *Solaris Essential Reference* is the reference you need when you know what you want to do and you just need to know how.

Linux System Administration
By M Carling and James T. Dennis
1st Edition Summer 1999
450 pages, $29.99
ISBN: 1-56205-934-3

As an administrator, you probably feel that most of your time and energy is spent in endless firefighting. If your network has become a fragile quilt of temporary patches and workarounds, then this book is for you. For example, have you had trouble sending or receiving your email lately?

Are you looking for a way to keep your network running smoothly with enhanced performance? Are your users always hankering for more storage, more services, and more speed? *Linux System Administration* advises you on the many intricacies of maintaining a secure, stable system. In this definitive work, the author addresses all the issues related to system administration, from adding users and managing files permission to Internet services and Web hosting to recovery planning and security. This book fulfills the need for expert advice that will ensure a trouble-free Linux environment.

Linux Enterprise Security
By John S. Flowers
1st Edition Fall 1999
400 pages, $39.99
ISBN: 0-7357-0035-4

New Riders is proud to offer the first book aimed specifically at Linux security issues. While there are a host of general UNIX security books, we thought it was time to address the practical needs of the Linux network. In this definitive work, author John Flowers takes a balanced approach to system security, from discussing topics like planning a secure environment to firewalls to utilizing security scripts. With comprehensive information on specific system compromises, and advice on how to prevent and repair them, this is one book that every Linux administrator should have on the shelf.

Development Titles

Developing Linux Applications

By Eric Harlow
1st Edition
400 pages, $34.99
ISBN: 0-7357-0021-4

We all know that Linux is one of the most powerful and solid operating systems in existence. And as the success of Linux grows, there is an increasing interest in developing applications with graphical user interfaces that really take advantage of the power of Linux. In this book, software developer Eric Harlow gives you an indispensable development handbook focusing on the GTK+ toolkit. More than an overview on the elements of application or GUI design, this is a hands-on book that delves deeply into the technology. With in-depth material on the various GUI programming tools and loads of examples, this book's unique focus will give you the information you need to design and launch professional-quality applications.

Linux Firewalls

By Robert Ziegler
Fall 1999
400 pages, $29.99
ISBN: 0-7357-0900-9

New Riders is proud to offer the first book aimed specifically at Linux security issues. While there are a host of general UNIX security books, we think it is time to address the practical needs of the Linux network. Author Robert Ziegler takes a balanced approach to system security, discussing topics like planning a secure environment, firewalls, and utilizing securtiy scripts. With comprehensive information on specific system compromises, and advice on how to prevent and repair them, this is one book that every Linux administrator should have on their shelf.

GTK+/Gnome Development

By Havoc Pennington
Summer 1999
400 pages, $34.99
ISBN: 0-7357-0078-8

GTK+ /Gnome Develpment provides the experienced programmer the knowledge to develop X Window applications with the powerful GTK+ toolkit. The author provides the reader with a checklist of features every application should have, advanced GUI techniques, and the ability to create custom widgets. The title also contains reference information for more experienced users already familiar with usage, but require knowledge of function prototypes and detailed descriptions. These tools let the reader write powerful applications in record time.

Python Essential Reference

By David Beazley
Fall 1999
270 pages, $34.95
ISBN: 0-7357-0901-7

This book describes the Python programming language and its library of standard modules. Python is an informal language that has become a highly valuable software development tool for many computing professionals. This language reference covers Python's lexical conventions, built-in datatypes, control flow, functions, statements, classes, and execution model. This book also covers the contents of the Python library as bundled in the standard Python distribution.

Lotus Notes and Domino Titles

Domino System Administration

By Rob Kirkland
1st Edition Fall 1999
500 pages, $39.99
ISBN: 1-56205-948-3

Your boss has just announced that you will be upgrading to the newest version of Notes and Domino when it ships. As a Premium Lotus Business Partner, Lotus has offered a substantial price break to keep your company away from Microsoft's Exchange Server. How are you supposed to get this new system installed, configured, and rolled out to all of your end users? You understand how Lotus Notes works—you've been administering it for years. What you need is a concise, practical explanation about the new features, and how to make some of the advanced stuff really work. You need answers and solutions from someone like you, who has worked with the product for years, and understands what it is you need to know. *Domino System Administration* is the answer—the first book on Domino that attacks the technology at the professional level, with practical, hands-on assistance to get Domino running in your organization.

Lotus Notes and Domino Essential Reference

By Dave Hatter & Tim Bankes
1st Edition
700 pages, $45.00
ISBN: 0-7357-0007-9

You're in a bind because you've been asked to design and program a new database in Notes for an important client that will keep track of and itemize a myriad of inventory and shipping data. The client wants a user-friendly interface, without sacrificing speed or functionality. You are experienced (and could develop this app in your sleep), but feel that you need to take your talents to the next level. You need something to facilitate your creative and technical abilities, something to perfect your programming skills. Your answer is waiting for you: *Lotus Notes and Domino Essential Reference.* It's compact and simply designed. It's loaded with information. All of the objects, classes, functions, and methods are listed. It shows you the object hierarchy and the overlaying relationship between each one. It's perfect for you. Problem solved.

Networking Titles

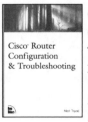

Cisco Router Configuration and Troubleshooting

Cisco Router Configuration & Troubleshooting

By Mark Tripod
1st Edition
300 pages, $34.99
ISBN: 0-7357-0024-9

Want the real story on making your Cisco routers run like a dream? Why not pick up a copy of *Cisco Router Configuration and Troubleshooting* and see what Mark Tripod has to say? His company is the one responsible for making some of the largest sites on the Net scream, like Amazon.com, Hotmail, USAToday, Geocities, and Sony. In this book, he provides advanced configuration issues, sprinkled with advice and preferred practices. You won't see a general overview on TCP/IP—we talk about more meaty issues like security, monitoring, traffic management, and more. In the troubleshooting section, Mark provides a unique methodology and lots of sample problems to illustrate. By providing real-world insight and examples instead of rehashing Cisco's documentation, Mark gives network administrators information they can start using today.

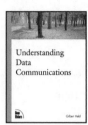

Understanding Data Communications, Sixth Edition

Understanding Data Communications

By Gilbert Held
6th Edition Summer 1999
550 pages, $34.99
ISBN: 0-7357-0036-2

Updated from the highly successful fifth edition, this book explains how data communications systems and their various hardware and software components work. Not an entry-level book, it approaches the material in a textbook format, addressing the complex issues involved in internetworking today. A great reference book for the experienced networking professional, written by noted networking authority, Gilbert Held.

New Riders

We Want to Know What You Think

To better serve you, we would like your opinion on the content and quality of this book. Please complete this card and mail it to us or fax it to 317-581-4663.

Name_____

Address _____

City _____State _____Zip _____

Phone _____

Email Address _____

Occupation _____

Operating System(s) that you use _____

What influenced your purchase of this book?

❑ Recommendation ❑ Cover Design
❑ Table of Contents ❑ Index
❑ Magazine Review ❑ Advertisement
❑ New Riders' Reputation ❑ Author Name

How would you rate the contents of this book?

❑ Excellent ❑ Very Good
❑ Good ❑ Fair
❑ Below Average ❑ Poor

How do you plan to use this book?

❑ Quick reference ❑ Self-training
❑ Classroom ❑ Other

What do you like most about this book?
Check all that apply.

❑ Content ❑ Writing Style
❑ Accuracy ❑ Examples
❑ Listings ❑ Design
❑ Index ❑ Page Count
❑ Price ❑ Illustrations

What do you like least about this book?
Check all that apply.

❑ Content ❑ Writing Style
❑ Accuracy ❑ Examples
❑ Listings ❑ Design
❑ Index ❑ Page Count
❑ Price ❑ Illustrations

What would be a useful follow-up book to this one for you? _____

Where did you purchase this book? _____

Can you name a similar book that you like better than this one, or one that is as good? Why?

_____

_____

How many New Riders books do you own? _____

What are your favorite computer books? _____

What other titles would you like to see us develop? _____

Any comments for us? _____

_____

_____

_____

Debian GNU/Linux: Guide to Installation and Usage, 0-7357-0914-9

Fold here and tape to mail

Place
Stamp
Here

New Riders Publishing
201 W. 103rd St.
Indianapolis, IN 46290

New Riders | How to Contact Us

Visit Our Web Site

www.newriders.com

On our Web site, you'll find information about our other books, authors, tables of contents, indexes, and book errata. You can also place orders for books through our Web site.

Email Us

Contact us at this address:

newriders@mcp.com

- If you have comments or questions about this book
- To report errors that you have found in this book
- If you have a book proposal to submit or are interested in writing for New Riders
- If you would like to have an author kit sent to you
- If you are an expert in a computer topic or technology and are interested in being a technical editor who reviews manuscripts for technical accuracy

newriders-sales@mcp.com

- To find a distributor in your area, please contact our international department at the address above.

newriders-pr@mcp.com

- For instructors from educational institutions who wish to preview New Riders books for classroom use. Email should include your name, title, school, department, address, phone number, office days/hours, text in use, and enrollment in the body of your text along with your request for desk/examination copies and/or additional information.

Write to Us

New Riders Publishing
201 W. 103rd St.
Indianapolis, IN 46290-1097

Call Us

Toll-free (800) 571-5840 + 9 + 7494
If outside U.S. (317) 581-3500. Ask for New Riders.

Fax Us

(317) 581-4663

This software is sold as is without warranty of any kind, either expressed or implied, including but not limited to the implied warranties of merchantability and fitness for a particular purpose. Neither the publisher nor its dealers or distributors assumes any liability for any alleged or actual damages arising from the use of this program. (Some states do not allow for the exclusion of implied warranties, so the exclusion may not apply to you.)

To run the enclosed CD, the minimum system requirement is a 386 processor with 4mg of RAM. To run X, the system requirement is a 486 processor with 16mg of RAM. 100mg of available hard drive space is needed for a base installation; 500mg to install X.